David Crystal is honorary professor of linguistics at the University of Bangor. He has written or edited over 100 books and published numerous articles for scholarly, professional, and general readerships, in fields ranging from forensic linguistics and ELT to the liturgy and Shakespeare. His books include the *Cambridge Encyclopedia of Language* (3rd edn 2010), *Just a Phrase I'm Going Through: My Life in Language* (Routledge, 2009), *The Fight for English* (OUP 2006) and *Fowler's Dictionary of Modern English Usage* (OUP, 2009).

RODIN THE TEXTER

Txtng
The Gr8 Db8

David Crystal
With cartoons by Ed McLachlan

OXFORD
UNIVERSITY PRESS

OXFORD
UNIVERSITY PRESS

Great Clarendon Street, Oxford OX2 6DP

Oxford University Press is a department of the University of Oxford.
It furthers the University's objective of excellence in research, scholarship,
and education by publishing worldwide in

Oxford New York

Auckland Cape Town Dar es Salaam Hong Kong Karachi Kuala Lumpur
Madrid Melbourne Mexico City Nairobi New Delhi Shanghai Taipei
Toronto

With offices in

Argentina Austria Brazil Chile Czech Republic France Greece
Guatemala Hungary Italy Japan South Korea Poland Portugal
Singapore Switzerland Thailand Turkey Ukraine Vietnam

Oxford is a registered trade mark of Oxford University Press
in the UK and in certain other countries

Published in the United States
by Oxford University Press Inc., New York

First Published 2008
First published in paperback 2009

British Library Cataloguing in Publication Data

Data available

Library of Congress Cataloging in Publication Data

Data available

Typeset by SPI Publisher Services, Pondicherry, India
Printed in Great Britain
on acid-free paper by
Clays Ltd, St Ives plc

ISBN 978-0-19-954490-5 (Hbk.)
      978-0-19-957133-8 (Pbk.)

10 9 8 7 6 5 4 3 2 1

Contents

Preface

Virtually every day I get an email or phone call – occasionally even a letter – from someone asking a linguistic question or wanting to share a linguistic observation. And over the past year or so I've noticed a trend: about half of these communications are about texting. For example, in May 2007 I received this from a journalist:

> Here in Orange County, California, 11 to 13-year-olds are increasingly using acronyms in their conversations. Text message shorthand is now everyday talk. Instead of exclaiming, 'Oh my god,' kids will say, 'OMG!' Instead of 'Just kidding,' they will say, 'JK.' I would like to know what you think of this development. Is it good or bad for language? Why is it happening? Has it happened before?

I put a brief response up on my blog.

As I was doing so, I searched for a general book which would answer these questions more fully. I couldn't find one. My own previous writing on this topic had been brief and anecdotal. Even in my *Language and the Internet* (2001), I devoted only a page or two to texting, as mobile phones were really off topic. And my *Glossary of Netspeak and Textspeak* (2004) was little more than a collection of usages, with no discussion of the issues raised by the journalist. A huge amount of research has been done on texting in the last ten years, but not much seems to have reached the general public.

It is the extraordinary antipathy to texting which has surprised me. I don't think I have ever come across a topic which has attracted more adult antagonism. I was sitting next to a lady at a literary lunch recently, who asked me what I was writing next. I told her about this book. 'I hate texting', she said. 'Why?' I asked. 'All those stupid abbreviations', she said. But (summarizing my Chapter 2) 'None of them are new,' I said. 'You played with abbreviations like those when you were a child. What have you got against them now?' 'I don't know,' she said. 'I just hate them.' And, realizing that this was an argument of the 'I love/hate modern art' type, I let the matter drop. I'd like to think, after reading this book, that she might change her mind – or, at least, come to realize that texting has values worth recognizing, even if she cannot appreciate them.

So there is clearly a topic to be debated, hence the sub-title to this book. But texting first of all needs to be described and explained. I first thought of writing a book on the subject in 2002, as a kind of sequel to my *Language and the Internet*; but the phenomenon was too recent. There was fascination and speculation a-plenty, but very little research into its linguistic character and function. Five years on, a large number of research reports have appeared, exploring text messaging from technological, sociological, psychological, commercial, and linguistic points of view, making it possible to start discussing its nature and purpose in a more informed and realistic way. *Txtng: The Gr8 Db8* is a linguist's take, as of 2008, on this rapidly evolving and highly intriguing topic.

Finally, I must acknowledge the help I have received from friends and colleagues in various parts of the world (listed in the Appendix) who have taken the trouble to compile lists of texting usage in their countries. Thanks to them, I have been able to give *Txtng* a much-needed multilingual perspective.

David Crystal
Holyhead

CHAPTER 1

The hype about texting

H ERE ARE EIGHT HEADLINES taken from a single page of research reports found on the Web in 2007.[1]

Texting fogs your brain like cannabis
Texting does not influence literacy skills
Texting replaces speech for communication among
    teenagers
Texting deprives children of sleep

Texting linked positively with literacy achievements
Texting helps shy teenagers communicate
Teenagers to get free mobiles to improve literacy
    standards
Mobiles prove effective in getting NEETs back
    into learning

NEETs? Those 'not currently engaged in employment, education, or training' – an acronym introduced following a UK government report in 2000.

We seem to have a problem. Has there ever been a linguistic phenomenon which has aroused such curiosity, suspicion, fear, confusion, antagonism, fascination, excitement, and enthusiasm, all at once? And in such a short space of time. Less than a decade ago, hardly anyone had heard of it.

The idea of a point-to-point short message service (or SMS) began to be discussed as part of the development

---

[1] The Web research reports were collected by the UK Literacy Trust: <http://www.literacytrust.org.uk/Database/texting.html>

of the Global System for Mobile Communications (or GSM) network in the mid-1980s, but it wasn't until the early 90s that phone companies started to develop the commercial possibilities. Texts communicated by pagers were replaced by text messages, at first only twenty characters in length. And although the first experimental messages were sent (in Finland) in 1992–3, it took five years or more before numbers of users started to build up. The average number of texts per GSM customer in 1995 was 0.4 per month; by the end of 2000 it was still only 35.[2]

The slow start, it seems, was because the companies had trouble working out reliable ways of charging for the new service. But once procedures were in place, texting rocketed. In the UK, in 2001, 12.2 billion (i.e. thousand million) text messages were sent. This had doubled by 2004, and was forecast to be 45 billion in 2007. On Christmas Day alone in 2006, over 205 million text messages went out. And that's just one country. World figures went from 17 billion in 2000 to 250 billion in 2001. They passed a trillion (million million) in 2005. Gartner, the industry analysts, predict the total will reach 2.4 trillion by 2010.[3] Given the lucrative nature of the business, a slowdown is inconceivable. Gartner reported that text messaging generated around

---

[2] GSM press release, 12 February 2001: <http://www.gsmworld.com/news/press_2001/press_releases_4.shtml>

[3] See www.gartner.com

70 billion dollars of revenue in 2005. That was over three times as much as all Hollywood box office sales that year.[4] The growth in usage has been a natural consequence of the phenomenal growth in penetration of the mobile phone (as it is known in British English – *mobile* for short), or cellphone (in American English – *cell*, for short). Although rates of diffusion vary greatly around the world, the common pattern is one of extraordinarily rapid growth. By 2003, Europe, Oceania, and North America each had more than one mobile subscription for every two people, and by 2007 several countries (such as Hong Kong, the UK, Sweden, and Italy) had passed saturation point, with the number of subscriptions equalling or exceeding the total population (due to many people taking out more than one subscription). China became the country with most subscriptions, passing 500 million in mid-2007. Africa was the fastest growing area in 2007, moving from 6 per cent to 21 per cent use within the population in the four years since 2003, and passing 200 million subscriptions mid-year. The accumulated estimates indicated that over 3 billion people, half the world's population, would have a mobile phone subscription by 2008.[5]

The technical properties of SMS define its communicative possibilities. One SMS message can contain up

---

[4] For statistics about usage, see <http://www.text.it/mediacentre/sms_figures.cfm>

[5] For these figures, see the following surveys and reports:

to 140 bytes (1,120 bits) of data. If characters (letters, punctuation marks, etc.) are encoded with 7 bits, as is usual for the Latin alphabet, then the maximum size of the message is 160 characters. If more complex symbols are to be represented (as in Chinese or Japanese writing), then a 16-bit Unicode encoding has to be used, and that reduces the size of the message to 70 characters. Besides text, an enhanced SMS system can also carry other kinds of data, such as ringtones, logos, and animations. It is even possible to send longer messages, using a system called 'concatenated SMS', which breaks a long message down into smaller chunks, sending them in sequence, though not all wireless devices support it. MMS (Multimedia Messaging Service) offers more ambitious options, including the transmission of photographs, sound files, video, and graphics, as well as longer messages.

Short messaging, short mail, SMSing, person-to-person messaging, mobile messaging, wireless messaging, text messaging, texting, txtng . . . whatever we call it, it is evidently here to stay. It is available on other systems, too, such as the Japanese DoCoMo i-mode service and the iPhone. So if it is causing problems, we

<http://www.bloomberg.com/apps/news?pid=20601080&sid=ahAcldNpX5no&refer=asia>
<http://www.ovum.com/go/content/c,377,70918>
<http://cn.w2forum.com/i/Hong_Kong_Has_The_Highest_Mobile_Phone_Penetration_In_Asia/related>
<http://www.forbes.com/finance/feeds/afx/2006/06/22/afx2832528.html>

need to be able to manage them. And if it is providing benefits, we need to know how to build on them. The surprising thing, for such a global phenomenon, is that so little reliable information about the language of texting has become public knowledge.[6] Psychologists, sociologists, health specialists, journalists, and educators have had plenty to say; but hardly any reports provide details of what exactly happens to language when people create texts. As a result, a huge popular mythology has grown up, in which exaggerated and distorted accounts of what youngsters are believed to do when they text has fuelled prophecies of impending linguistic disaster.

The popular belief is that texting has evolved as a twenty-first-century phenomenon – as a highly distinctive graphic style, full of abbreviations and deviant uses of language, used by a young generation that doesn't care about standards. There is a widely voiced concern that the practice is fostering a decline in literacy. And some even think it is harming language as a whole. 'Text messages destroying our language', headed

---

[6] There is a valuable online bibliography at <http://socrates.berkeley.edu/%7Enalinik/mobile/articles.html>
See also Manuel Castells, Mireia Fernandez-Ardevol, and Jack Linchuan Qiu, *The Mobile Communication Society: A cross-cultural analysis of available evidence on the social uses of wireless communication technology.* Research report prepared for the International Workshop on Wireless Communication Policies and Prospects: A Global Perspective (University of Southern California: Annenberg School for Communication, 2004). <http://arnic.info/WirelessWorkshop/MCS.pdf>

a report in a Washington paper in May 2007, and the writer goes on:[7]

> I knew this was coming. From the first time one of
> my friends sent me the message 'I've got 2 go, talk to
> U later,' I knew the end was near. The English language
> as we once knew it is out the window, and replacing
> it is this hip and cool slang-induced language, obsessed
> with taking the vowels out of words and spelling
> fonetikally.

Crispin Thurlow, a linguist at the University of Washington, has collected dozens of such reports, which cumulatively have generated a sense of 'moral panic' in the population.[8] There is now a widespread folk belief that, whatever texting is, it must be a bad thing.

It isn't just the USA that is panicking. In the UK, also in 2007, broadcaster John Humphrys exploded in the *Daily Mail*. In an article headed 'I h8 txt msgs: How texting is wrecking our language', he uses some of the most apocalyptic language I have ever read to condemn it. Texters are:

---

[7] Eric Uthus, 7 May 2007: <http://www.thedaily.washington.edu/article/2007/5/7/textMessagesDestroyingOurLanguage>

[8] Crispin Thurlow, 'From statistical panic to moral panic: the metadiscursive construction and popular exaggeration of new media language in the print media', *Journal of Computer-Mediated Communication* 11 (3). <http://jcmc.indiana.edu/vol11/issue3/thurlow.html>
The term 'moral panic' is the watchword of Stan Cohen, *Folk Devils and Moral Panics* (Routledge, 1972, 3rd edn 2002).

vandals who are doing to our language what Genghis
Khan did to his neighbours eight hundred years ago.
They are destroying it: pillaging our punctuation;
savaging our sentences; raping our vocabulary. And
they must be stopped.[9]

The end is nigh! If I had a pound for every time I have
heard of someone predicting a language disaster because of a new technological development, I should be
a very rich man. My bank balance would have started
to grow with the arrival in the Middle Ages of printing,
thought by many to be the invention of the devil
because it would put all kinds of false opinions into
people's minds. It would have increased with the arrival of the telegraph, telephone, and broadcasting,
each of which generated short-lived fears that the fab-
ric of society was under threat. And I would have been
able to retire on the profits from text messaging, the
latest innovation to bring out the prophets of doom.

All the popular beliefs about texting are wrong, or
at least debatable. Its graphic distinctiveness is not a
totally new phenomenon. Nor is its use restricted to
the young generation. There is increasing evidence that
it helps rather than hinders literacy. And only a very
tiny part of the language uses its distinctive orthography. A trillion text messages may seem a lot, but

when we set these alongside the multi-trillion instances of standard orthography in everyday life, they appear as no more than a few ripples on the surface of the sea of language. Texting has added a new dimension to language use, indeed, but its long-term impact on the already existing varieties of language is likely to be negligible. It is not a bad thing.

That is my flag nailed to the mast. All these issues need a thoroughgoing exploration. And I begin with the basic question: What actually takes place, linguistically speaking, when people text each other? The answer contains a few surprises.

CHAPTER 2

How weird is texting?

THE POPULAR IMPRESSION, created largely by the media, is that the written language encountered on mobile phone screens is weird. It has been labelled 'textese', 'slanguage', a 'new hi-tech lingo', a 'hybrid shorthand', a 'digital virus'. It has been described as 'foreign', 'alien', and 'outlandish'. It is so much viewed as a new language that texters have been called 'bilingual'. And what does this new fluency communicate? Nothing much, according to one commentator:[1]

> As a dialect, text ('textese'?) is thin and – compared, say, with Californian personalised licence plates – unimaginative. It is bleak, bald, sad shorthand. Drab shrinktalk.... The dialect has a few hieroglyphs (codes comprehensible only to initiates) and a range of face symbols.... Linguistically it's all pig's ear.... it masks dyslexia, poor spelling and mental laziness. Texting is penmanship for illiterates.

As far as I know I am not dyslexic, mentally lazy, or illiterate. But I text.

That quotation is taken from a British newspaper, *The Guardian*, in 2002. It was very early days to be passing such a savage judgement on a use of language only a few years old. And especially odd to see it in the *Guardian*, which the year before had held the first

---

[1] John Sutherland, 'Cn u txt?' *Guardian Unlimited*, 11 November 2002 <http://www.guardian.co.uk/mobile/article/0,2763,837709,00.html> But see now fn. 16 on p. 33.

text-messaging poetry competition, which gave the lie to everything that this commentator was asserting.

The requirement was to write a poem within the 160-character constraint of the mobile phone screen. It proved a popular idea. In the first year there were nearly 7,500 entries. The poems were judged by a panel which included poets Peter Sansom and U. A. Fanthorpe. These are the two top entries, from Hetty Hughes (who won first prize) and Steve Kilgallon.[2]

> txtin iz messin,
> mi headn'me englis,
> try2rite essays,
> they all come out txtis.
> gran not plsed w/letters shes getn,
> swears i wrote better
> b4 comin2uni.
> &she's african

> Sheffield
> Sun on maisonette windows
> sends speed-camera flashes tinting through tram cables
> startling drivers
> dragging rain-waterfalls in their wheels
> I drive on

Hardly drab shrinktalk. Peter Sansom commented:

---

[2] <http://technology.guardian.co.uk/online/story/0,3605,481985,00.html>

One of the joys of the competition was how much grainy real-life could be got into 160 characters, though there was room for delicate watercolour too.

And U. A. Fanthorpe affirmed:

I was moved and amazed at how much feeling could be introduced in so small a space: there was great tenderness, spirit, imagination in the best entries.

This is light years away from any concept of 'bleak, bald, sad shorthand'.

Plainly there is more going on here than in the stereotyped conception of texting presented by the *Guardian* commentator. From an orthographic point of view, the two poems are strikingly different, and this makes the first and most important point about texting: nobody says you *have* to use abbreviated language – and three out of the top five poems didn't. It is an option. Indeed, the *Guardian* competition recognized this by giving a special prize to the most creative use of SMS 'shorthand', as they put it. It went to Julia Bird. (Some readers may need the gloss, in this instance.)

14: a txt msg pom.	14: a text message poem.
his is r bunsn brnr bl%,	his eyes are bunsen burner blue,
his hair lyk fe filings	his hair like iron filings
W/ac/dc going thru.	with ac/dc going through.
I sit by him in kemistry,	I sit by him in chemistry,

| it splits my @oms | it splits my atoms |
| wen he :-)s @ me. | when he smiles at me. |

This is obviously much more orthographically innovative than the poem which got first prize. Indeed, on first glance it seems to be totally deviant. But actually it still retains several features of the standard language. *I* is written with a capital letter; five of the seven lines end with a punctuation mark; and *fe*, *ac*, and *dc* are standard abbreviations. More surprising – for our first impression is to the contrary – of the thirty-four words in the poem, over half (eighteen) are in standard English spelling. In three of the lines (3, 5, 6) there is only *one* small spelling change.

Where does the impression of total deviance come from? It is the distinctive spellings and symbols which take up all our attention, so that we fail to notice the 'normal' elements elsewhere. To say that this poem is written in a 'foreign language', as many media commentators would, is highly misleading: visually, it is over half the same as in its traditional representation. And grammatically, it is straightforward standard English, as the glossed version shows.

The judges gave Julia the prize for special text creativity. In fact, Hetty's supposedly less innovative poem is in some respects more deviant. Hetty writes the first-person pronoun as *i*, she runs more words together, her grammar is more elliptical, and only ten of its twenty-seven words are in standard spelling. But her text gives the impression of being more conventional because she avoids the use of emoticons (such as :-)) and special typographic symbols (such as @) – features I will discuss in detail in Chapter 3.

In any collection of text messages, it is the combination of standard and nonstandard features which is the most striking characteristic – and with good reason. Although many young texters like to be different, and enjoy breaking the rules, they also know they need to be understood. There is no point in paying for a message if it breaks so many rules of a language that it ceases to be intelligible. So there is always an unconscious pressure to respect some of the standard properties of the orthography.

Often the texter has little choice. Take line 3 of Julia's poem, which is in standard English spelling apart from the word *lyk* 'like'. How would you shorten *hair* yet still preserve its recognizability? *Har*? *Hir*? *Her*? *Hr*? What would you do with *filings*? *Flings*? *Flngs*? *Filngs*? These abbreviations would be extremely difficult to decode, especially as the meaning of the sentence lacks predictability. This is not a sentence of the kind 'Am on the train', where it would be possible to shorten *train* to *trn* because the sender knows that the receiver is aware of the context. Comparing hair to iron filings is of a rather different expressive order.

Another tiny feature of Hetty's poem is worth noting – in the line *&she's african*. It is the use of the apostrophe. Try keying in an apostrophe on a mobile phone: on my phone it takes four keystrokes – one to access the set of punctuation marks, two to get to the apostrophe, and one more to transfer it to the screen. On some phones, it might take as many as six keystrokes. This is hardly a rapid or easy convention to introduce into a text, so the fact that it is used at all is a clear indication of the texter's underlying respect for traditional expectations. Apostrophes are surprisingly frequent. In one American study of 544 messages, apostrophes turned up in as many as 192 instances (35 per cent).[3] This finding at least should give some reassurance to members of the Apostrophe Protection Society.

The use of apostrophes is interesting, because it involves more than just a matter of maintaining intelligibility. There are actually very few cases in English where the omission of an apostrophe causes genuine misunderstanding (the apostrophe is a quite recent innovation in the writing system). The contracted form *we're* is a case in point: typed without the apostrophe, it could be misread as *were*. But there is no ambiguity with *Im*, *shes*, or *theyre*, for example; and the context, along with the place of the word in the sentence,

---

[3] Crispin Thurlow with Alex Brown, 'Generation Txt? The sociolinguistics of young people's text-messaging', *Discourse Analysis Online*, 2003. <http://extra.shu.ac.uk/daol/articles/v1/n1/a3/thurlow2002003–01.html>

invariably makes it clear whether a texter means *we'd* or *wed*, *can't* or *cant*, *we'll* or *well*, and so on. Similarly, context usually helps us decide whether we mean *cats* or *cat's* or *cats'*. So, if there is no strict need most of the time to have apostrophes in order to guarantee comprehension, the only reason texters put them in must be as an aid to clarity, to maintain the familiar appearance of the orthography so that it becomes easier to read. It would certainly take fractionally longer for the brain to process and interpret *&shes african*.

In everyday texting situations, where the poetic motivation is less strong (though not entirely absent, as we shall see later), the tacit respect for the standard conventions of the writing system is even more striking. Here is a small selection of messages, chosen to illustrate the range of styles people use.

U 2. Glad journey OK. x
what R U sayin?
Landed safely. On way to town. xxx
c u in 5 min x
what tim does th trn gt in?
let me know if u want me 2 pick u up
U miss me? ;-)
i'll b there by 7
we've just had a drink with Jon!!!!

All of these texters were literate people; they knew how to spell *are*, *you*, *seven*, and so on. The fact that they chose not to use the conventional spelling thus needs explaining. What do texters think they are doing, when they write in this way? That's a question I shall answer in Chapter 4.

When messages are longer, containing more information, the amount of standard orthography tends to increase. Many texters alter just the grammatical words (such as *you*, *be* and *can*), as in this example

> if u cn send me the disk by post i'll get it copied. make sure u get a receipt 4 it so tht we cn claim the cost of the postage back.

As older and more conservative language users begin to text, an even more standardized style appears. Some people refuse to depart from traditional orthography – but they still text. Their texts may use quite informal language, but they are nonetheless spelled, capitalized, and punctuated conventionally.

> I'll pick up your mum on the way to your place, if that's OK? We ought to be at the theatre by 6 latest.

And conventional spelling and punctuation is the norm when institutions send out alert messages, as in this university text to students:

> Weather Alert! No classes today due to snow storm.

or in the texts which radio listeners are invited to send in to programmes.

The impression one quickly gets from any random sample of texts is how stylistically diverse they are. It is partly a matter of age and familiarity (or lack of it) with the medium – a pattern that has also been observed with some of the other kinds of electronic communication, such as emails. When email began, young geeks broke rules of spelling, capitalization, and punctuation with gay abandon, and their daring style became fashionable. But as email spread throughout the population, its style evolved to reflect the linguistic habits of the users, many of whom were comfortable only in standard English. Diversity is now the e-norm. Among my recent emails is one which begins 'Yo, DC' and another which begins 'Revered Professor'. And a wide spectrum of usage in the use of capital letters and punctuation can be observed.[4]

But age is not the only factor. Gender differences are apparent in all sort of ways, as we shall see in Chapter 5: for example, women use more exclamation marks than men.[5] Regional and ethnic dialect differences emerge, especially in spellings that reflect local pronunciations, such as *wiv* 'with' or *wassup* 'what's up' (see p. 49). And fashion has an important role to play, especially among

---

[4] Many of these are reviewed in my *Language and the Internet* (Cambridge: CUP, 2006), chapter 4.

[5] Carol Waseleski, 'Gender and the use of exclamation points in computer-mediated communication: An analysis of exclamations posted to two electronic discussion lists', *Journal of Computer-Mediated Communication*, 11(4), 2006. <http://jcmc.indiana.edu/vol11/issue4/waseleski.html>

young texters. Some 'older' teenagers now seek to distance themselves from the use of emoticons, such as :), in their texts, believing them to be childish or uncool.

The research studies have made it perfectly clear that the early media hysteria about the novelty (and thus the dangers) of text messaging was misplaced. Take the belief I illustrated on page 8, that youngsters are 'obsessed with taking the vowels out of words'. In the American study referred to above, less than 20 per cent of the corpus of text messages displayed abbreviated forms of any kind – about three per message. And in a Norwegian study, the proportion was even lower, with just 6 per cent of texts using abbreviations.[6] Hardly any non-alphabetic symbols were used, apart from *x* and *!*, which often appeared in sequences (as *xxxx* in farewells, for example). Emoticons were unusual. And, surprisingly, so were combinations of letters and numbers (such as *gr8* 'great') – surprising, because it is this feature of texting which is given such a high profile in the media and which tends to be most satirized. If a newspaper uses a jokey headline about texting, almost certainly a word like *gr8* will be in it. I wouldn't be surprised to find it in a book title one day.

---

[6] 'The socio-linguistics of SMS: An analysis of SMS use by a random sample of Norwegians', in R. Ling and P. Pedersen (eds), *Mobile Communications: Renegotiation of the Social Sphere* (London: Springer, 2005), 335–49. The low use of abbreviations and emoticons is also reported by Ylve Hård af Segerstad, 'Use and adaptations of written language to the conditions of computer-mediated communication', PhD Dept of Linguistics, Göteborg University, 2002, 200. Other samples occasionally show a higher proportion, but I have never seen any sample go above 20 per cent.

The highly distinctive text messages which attract media publicity are not typical of the genre as a whole. Part of the problem, I suspect, was the way in which internet enthusiasts, impressed by the way abbreviated forms and emoticons were being used in early email and chatroom interactions, compiled dictionaries and brochures to introduce people to what was being presented as a 'new language'. Andy Ihnatko's online dictionary, *Cyberspeak*, is an example.[7] Another is 'The Byte-Sized Guide to E-mail', a free leaflet circulated by the UK telecommunications firm BT in the late 1990s, in which we find such statements as 'e-mail is a hotbed of abbreviations', and including such examples as TANSTAAFL ('There ain't no such thing as a free lunch'). Its list of fourteen sample emoticons includes 7:-), glossed 'baseball cap'.

These collections are interesting in showing the lengths to which people go when they are playing with language, but there is no way of knowing whether a particular usage is rare or common, a one-off or a standard form. This sequence appears in some collections, for example:

ROTFL	rolling on the floor laughing
ROTFLMAO	rolling on the floor laughing my ass off

---

[7] Andy Ihnatko, *Cyberspeak: An Online Dictionary* (New York: Random House, 1997).

ROTFLMAOAY	rolling on the floor laughing my ass off at you
ROTFLMAOWTIME	rolling on the floor laughing my ass off with tears in my eyes

It seems unlikely that such long sequences would ever be used in real text messages. And why anyone would want to talk so much about baseball caps in the first place – and in the UK, too – is a point which seems to have escaped the compilers.

The published lists of abbreviations and emoticons are extensive – over 500 in each category have been recorded. Probably less than 5 per cent of them are ever used. But this has not stopped people swallowing whole the stories that appear from time to time in the press, asserting that youngsters use nothing else when they text. For example, in 2003 a story was widely reported that a teenager had written an essay entirely in textspeak, which her teacher was 'totally unable to understand'. As no-one was ever able to track down the entire essay, it may well have been a hoax – or at least a clever case of 'trying it on', the linguistic equivalent of walking into class wearing a hoodie. Certainly, the extract which appeared in all the reports had very little in common with the everyday texting patterns noted above. It rather resembled the poetry cases, as a contrived attempt to maximize the distinctiveness of the genre, and it displayed a considerable level of linguistic ingenuity. The reported extract began like this:

> My smmr hols wr CWOT. B4, we used 2go2 NY 2C
> my bro, his GF & thr 3 :-@ kids FTF. ILNY, it's
> a gr8 plc.

And it was translated like this:

> My summer holidays were a complete waste of time.
> Before, we used to go to New York to see my brother,
> his girlfriend and their three screaming kids face to
> face. I love New York. It's a great place.

If I'd been the teacher, I would have given the student 10 out of 10 for her linguistic ingenuity, and 0 out of 10 for her sense of appropriateness (or alternatively, 10 out of 10 for cheek). I shall discuss the educational issues further in Chapter 8.

This is perhaps as near as we might get to the 'foreign language' conception of texting. Even so, it is worth noting that the sentences use (informal) stand-ard English grammar. The second sentence is really quite complex, with its careful use of tense forms, coordination, and word order. Ten of the words are spelled normally (eleven, if we include the ampersand). *Hols* and *bro* are common colloquialisms outside of texting. Most of us would have no trouble reading in the missing vowels in *summer*, though we might pause a moment over *wr*, *thr*, and *plc*. And no-one would have difficulty with 'translating' such forms as *2* as 'to', for this – as we shall see in Chapter 3 – is a well-established convention of rebus games. The only real problems are the acronyms – *CWOT*, *GF*, and *FTF*, and perhaps *NY* and *ILNY* for people living outside the USA. But difficulties with acronyms are by no means restricted to texting. They pose problems in any context where we are unfamiliar with the subject-matter:

> The PHCT are going to be looking at the CRS with the CPO.

That is: 'The Primary Health Care Team are going to be looking at the Client Record System with the Chief Pharmaceutical Officer'. I found this in an internal hospital memorandum.

Even with the more extreme cases of abbreviation, the problem of unintelligibility is far less than some have suggested. As one texter said:

> f u cn rd ths thn wats th prblm?

Texters have evidently intuited a basic principle of information theory: that consonants carry much more information than vowels. We are unused to vowelless writing in English, but it is a perfectly normal system in several languages, such as Arabic and Hebrew. And even in English there have been many demonstrations to show that a piece of text with vowels omitted is intelligible, whereas one with consonants omitted is not:

ths sntnc hsnt gt ny vwls.

i eee a o a ooa. [= this sentence hasn't got any consonants]

We can handle consonant writing. And it turns out we can handle the other distinctive features of texting orthography too. People were playing with language in this way long before mobile phones were invented. Texting may be using a new technology, but its linguistic processes are centuries old.

The novelty of texting means that people are in the early stages of working out the rules which should govern its forms and functions – as indeed they still are with email and chat. Informal etiquette guides are being compiled.[8] They make such recommendations as:

Don't text when you're with someone else, without apology
Don't text if you've had too much to drink
Don't text while driving
Don't say anything in text you wouldn't say in person
Don't send bad news by text

But these are prescriptions, not guidelines based on what people actually do. In fact, in relation to the last prescription, several instances have been reported of texts being used to send bad news – for instance, to

---

[8] For example: <http://www.wirelessdevnet.com/newswire-less/thefeature04.html> <http://geeksugar.com/192089>

tell the recipient that the sender is ending a relationship, divorcing, or firing. The issue of divorce became controversial as early as 2001, when cases were reported of Muslim men divorcing their wives by saying 'I divorce you' three times (as required by Islamic law) – but by SMS.[9] In some countries, such as Malaysia and Singapore, an initial legal sanction of the practice caused such an outcry that the decision was quickly revoked. And in 2003, workers at a British factory learned that they had been made redundant when they received notice of dismissal by text.[10] The internet provides many more examples, though one must be cautious about accepting everything one reads there at face value.

We are still learning how to behave when we text. Which messages require a response and which do not? The norm seems to be that a quick response is expected; failure to respond is seen as a situation requiring special treatment.[11] Most commonly, the sender sends exactly the same message again, assuming that there has been a transmission error. Other strategies are to follow the first message up with a different one; or to switch medium, making a phone call. Several factors can be present: the recipient might be temporarily unavailable;

---

[9] <http://www.textually.org/textually/archives/2003/07/001235.htm>
<http://www.altmuslim.com/perm.php?id=1056_0_26_0_C25>

[10] <http://www.theinquirer.net/default.aspx?article=9769>

[11] Response times: Ditte Laursen, 'Please reply! The replying norm in adolescent SMS communication', in R. Harper, L. Palen, and A. Taylor (eds), *The Inside Text: Social, Cultural and Design Perspectives in SMS* (Dordrecht: Springer, 2005), 53–73.

the content or expression of the message might be unpalatable; the relationship between the sender and the recipient might be breaking down. If a response is slow in forthcoming, there is an expectation by the sender of an apology or excuse from the recipient. Very few text messages do not require a response – chain messages and news alerts, for example, or messages sent last thing at night. Senders also usually take time-zone differences into account, when judging whether an immediate response is likely.

The changes in our communicative behaviour, and in our expectations about the communicative behaviour of others, are quite striking. Mizuko Ito and Daisuke Okabe, in a study of young Japanese messaging, put it like this:[12]

> While mobile phones have become a vehicle for youths
> to challenge the power-geometries of places such as
> the home, and the street, they have also created new
> disciplines and power-geometries, the need to be
> continuously available to friends and lovers, and the
> need to always carry a functioning mobile device.
> These disciplines are accompanied by new sets of
> social expectations and manners. When unable to
> return a message right away, young people feel that
> a social expectation has been violated.

[12] Mizuko Ito and Daisuke Okabe, 'Intimate connections: contextualizing Japanese youth and mobile messaging', in R. Harper, L. Palen, and A. Taylor (see note 11), 139.

This state of affairs can be encountered in any country. Text messaging seems to have increased our expectation that we are mutually accessible.

Several of Norman Silver's poems provide an insight into a texter's world view. In 'the old old days', one texter tries to sort out in his mind how things were before mobiles arrived:[13]

in the old old days
b4 there were mobile fones
how cud a boy eva meet
a person of the oppsite gender

& even if they cud get acquainted
wivout a mobile fone
how cud they ch@
each uvver up

& even if they cud natter
wivout a mobile fone
how cud they stay in touch
if they were in diffrent classes

& even if they cud communic8
wivout a mobile fone
how cud they flirt
or get 2 kno each uvver

[13] Norman Silver, *Age, Sex, Location* (Colchester: tXt café, 2006).

& even if they cud get close
wivout a mobile fone
how cud they say gudnite
@bedtime

And his poem continues for another fifteen stanzas of puzzlement.

A different mood is evoked in 'dpressd':

nobody is txting me
im troubld & im stressd
wen no one even thinks of me
it makes me feel dpressd

my mates r probly having fun
while im fed up & bored
waiting 4 an sms
th@ proves im not ignored ...

The writer talks sadly about her state for another three stanzas, before we read:

shud i charge the battery
in case its lost its power?
no ones txtd me 4 yonx
it must b ½ an hour!

If there are issues here, they are for sociology and psychology to explore, not linguistics.

The problem for linguists will be how to keep up with the technology. New ways of displaying messages, such as on the iPhone, will affect the dynamic of texting, motivating longer dialogues containing shorter messages (along the lines of instant messaging). Also, the increased use of group-based text-messaging systems is bound to be an important factor in influencing norms of usage. In addition, they have to cope with the fact that texting is an instance of a variety of language in very rapid evolution. Unlike the well-established varieties of language, text messaging has still to become codified. There is no 'house style' for texting, as there is in writing for newspapers or journals. Many linguistic variants exist. A word like *maybe* might be written in several ways – I have seen *mayb, mybe, myb, mab, mAB, mabe*, and *mAbe*.

Similarly, it is not yet clear how far variant types of text messaging will emerge. As we shall see in Chapter 6, the different functions of texting (in greetings, rapport, word-play, alerts, and so on) motivate different kinds of language. Some use abbreviated forms, some don't. Some use full sentences; some don't. Some engage in word-play; some don't. Differences have been noted between the sexes and between people with different regional, social, and occupational backgrounds. Differences have been noted between youngsters and adults. There are many variables, and they need to be explored before we can be confident we understand what people do when they text.

It is too early to say just how much impact texting will have on speech – the question posed by my correspondent in my Preface. I have heard teenagers say *lol* 'laughing out loud' (pronounced both as 'lol' and 'ell oh ell'), *omg* 'oh my God', and *jk* 'just kidding', and evidently some young texting champions routinely talk that way.[14] A 2007 commercial for Cingular on US television, usually called 'My bff Jill', achieved cult status, prompting several parodies on YouTube: it shows a mother complaining about the phone bill to her daughter, who replies mainly in text abbreviations (such as *bff* = 'best friend forever') which the mother does her best to keep up with.[15] The contributors to the associated YouTube forum make it clear that several textisms are fashionable in young people's speech. And the other day I heard an adult say *imho* 'in my humble opinion'. Most of these innovations will probably die away; but some may live on, and add new acronyms to the spoken language.

[14] <http://www.smh.com.au/news/phones-pdas/fyi-13yo-skool-grl-nu-us-txt-chmpn-us/2007/04/23/1177180533175.html>

[15] <http://www.youtube.com/watch?v=4nIUcRJX9-o>

[16] John Sutherland provided me with an excellent hook to start my argument in this chapter (p. 00); but, as he pointed out in a review of this book in the *New Statesman* (4 August 2008), his remarks were made some years ago, and his views 'have undergone a Kuhnian paradigm shift' since then. His 2004 campaign with dot.mobile aimed at integrating texting into education, and he's been an advocate of the educational use of texting in various contexts since. Other critics of the medium should take note.

Texting, he now believes, has its uses, though he gives it only ten years before obsolescence. Having seen the way Barack Obama used it in his election campaign, and noting the way organizations of all kinds are increasingly using it to keep in touch with their supporters, I think it's going to be around a lot longer than that. More on this in Chapter 6.

CHAPTER 3

What makes texting distinctive?

THERE ARE SEVERAL DISTINCTIVE FEATURES of the way texts are written which combine to give the impression of novelty that so attracts the attention of media commentators. I identify six main kinds in this chapter. But none of them is in fact linguistically novel. In each case we can find antecedents in earlier language use. Many of them were being used in computer interactions that predated the arrival of mobile phones, such as in chatrooms. Some can be found in pre-computer informal writing, dating back a hundred years or more. And some are very ancient indeed.

Pictograms and logograms

Let me begin with what is evidently the most noticeable feature of text orthography – the use of single letters, numerals, and typographic symbols to represent words, parts of words, or even – as in the case of x and z – noises associated with actions:

b	be
2	to
@	at
x	'kiss'

When graphic units are used in this way, they are technically known as *logograms* or *logographs* – or, in the case of some languages (such as Chinese) *characters*.

Logograms in texting may be used alone, or in combination:

b4	before
@oms	atoms
2day	today
xxx	'kisses'
zzz	'sleeping'

It is the pronunciation of the logogram which is the critical thing, not the visual shape. That is the essential difference with the graphic devices called *emoticons* (or *smileys*), where the meaning is entirely a function of the shape of the symbols (when read sideways, with the head to the left):

:-)	'smile'
;-)	'wink'
:-@	'screaming'
@(---`---`---	'rose'

(or read straight ahead, as in Japanese and some other East Asian systems):

(*o*)	'surprised'
(^_^)	'cute'

When visual shapes, or pictures, are used to represent objects or concepts, they are known as *pictograms* or *pictographs*. Emoticons are a type of pictogram. Although several hundred have been devised, most fall under the category of 'computer art' (such as the rose above). Very few are used in texting, and none of them with any great frequency. (They are much more common in instant messaging, where the computer software allows easy and immediate access using prepared icons; there are 64 emoticons readily available for use in a Skype conversation, for example.)

The commentator I quoted on page 13 talked disparagingly about 'hieroglyphs', but the symbols found in texting are not like the writing system of Ancient Egypt. Egyptian hieroglyphs were complex entities, combinations of symbols representing both concepts and sounds. Only rarely in texting do we see such combinations – there happens to be an example in Hetty's poem (p. 16), where she writes 'smiles' as :-)s, but this is unusual. Normally, the letters and logograms of texting inhabit a totally different space from that of pictograms. The @ in the word @*om* and the @ in the emoticon of 'screaming' may look the same, but they perform completely different functions. In the first case, you listen to its sound; in the second case, you look at its shape.

But there *is* a point of similarity between texting and Egyptian writing: the notion of a *rebus*. A rebus is a message which, in its original definition, consists entirely of pictures that are used to represent the sounds of words, rather than the objects they refer to. For example, the picture of a bee can in English be 'read' as either *bee* or *be*. Followed by the letters *st,* the sequence of picture + letters can be read as *beast*. A carving in a church at Kidlington in Oxfordshire shows a kid (goat), a ling (fish), and a ton of wool. Many place names, person names, and heraldic emblems use rebuses in this way.

The kind of rebuses which I remember from childhood Christmas annuals were puzzles which mixed pictures and logograms. Thus we might find:

numeral + picture + picture + picture + numeral + picture					
2	of a bee	of an oar	of a knot	2	of a bee

This, we would be told, was a 'well-known phrase or saying'. Modern incarnations of this procedure we find in such television game-shows as *Concentration* (in the US) and *Catchphrase* (in the UK). Another old example is this one, made up entirely (apart from the last word) of letter and numeral logograms:

YY U R YY U B I C U R YY 4 ME
'too wise you are ...'

Really tricky combinations can be found in such commercial party games as *Dingbats*.

Rebuses have an ancient history. The word comes from a Latin tag *non verbis sed rebus* – 'not with words but with things'. They are known in Latin, and found in European art and literature. Leonardo da Vinci drew rebus puzzles. Ben Jonson ridiculed them in one of his plays. They were especially popular in the nineteenth century. Lewis Carroll put them into his letters to children. The earliest use in English seems to be in 1605, when the antiquarian William Camden referred to people who 'lackt wit to expresse their conceit in speech; did vse to depaint it out (as it were) in pictures, which they call Rebus'.

So there is actually nothing novel at all about such text messages as *c u l8r* in English or *7ac* in French ('set ah say' = *c'est assez*). They are part of the European ludic linguistic tradition, and doubtless analogues can be found in all languages which have been written down. Individual texters may have devised some of the modern abbreviations without being aware of that tradition, but they are only doing what generations have done before them. And certainly there should be no reason for us to be taken aback when we encounter such forms in texting, for we have all seen them before. To suggest that they are part of a 'code for initiates' is to ignore linguistic history.

Initialisms

Probably the second most noticeable feature of texting is the reduction of words to their initial letters – what are known as *initialisms*. Initialisms are familiar in proper names, such as *NATO* and *BBC*. They are often called *acronyms* (though some people restrict that term to the forms that are pronounced as single words, such as *NATO*, calling forms such as *BBC alphabetisms*). What happens in texting – as indeed in other forms of computer-mediated communication, such as instant messaging – is that everyday words, rather than proper names, are reduced to their initial letters. I illustrate using capitalized forms, but any example can appear in upper- or lower-case.

We find initials used for individual words:

N no   *G* grin   *Q* queue   *W* with   *Y* yes

for elements of compound words:

GF girlfriend   *DL* download   *W/E* weekend

for words in phrases:

CWOT	complete waste of time	*FTF*	face to face
NP	no problem	*AML*	all my love

for words in elliptical or whole sentences:

JK Just kidding   *DK* Don't know   *CMB* Call me back
SWDYT So what do you think?
MMYT Mail me your thoughts

and for words in expostulations:

OMG Oh my God!   *AB* Ah bless!
YYSSW Yeah, yeah, sure, sure, whatever!

As with logograms and emoticons, popular accounts tend to overestimate the range and frequency of initialisms in texting. Only a very few, such as LOL ('laughing out loud', also used for 'lots of love') are used repeatedly. Most are idiosyncratic embellishments designed to show that the texter knows how to play the texting game, as in the ROTFL sequence on page 23.

As with logograms, the examples may be new, but the process is not. People have been initializing common phrases for centuries. The Latin initialism *pm* (*post meridiem* 'after midday') is first recorded in English in 1666; *NB* (*nota bene* 'note well'), in 1673. *IOU* is known from 1618. In the nineteenth century we find *RIP* ('rest in peace') and *ND* ('no date'). In the early twentieth we have *AWOL* ('absent without leave'), *NBG* ('no bloody good'), and *SWALK* ('sealed with a loving kiss'). The mid-century produced such forms as *ETA* ('estimated time of arrival'), *SNAFU* ('situation normal, all fouled/fucked up'), *AKA* ('also known as'), and the famous *TTFN* ('ta-ta for now'), used by the Cockney charlady Mrs Mopp in the BBC radio series *ITMA* ('It's That Man Again'). Everyone used this last one in my house when I was a child.

These examples could be multiplied: *FYI* ('for your information'), *ASAP* ('as soon as possible'), *MD* ('doctor of medicine' or 'managing director'), *NA* ('not applicable')... Many initialisms have been used in specialized contexts, such as *VGC* ('very good condition' in antiquarianism), *LBW* ('leg before wicket' in cricket), *ERA* ('earned run average' in baseball), *C/O* ('care of' in postal addressing), *H&C* ('hot and cold' in accommodation), *APR* ('annual percentage rate' in economics), *NNE* ('north-north-east' in geography). Some have become so familiar that people forget their original status as initialisms (*CD, DVD, AIDS*) and may even be unable to say what the letters originally stood for, as in the case of *laser* ('light amplification by the stimulated emission of radiation').

The practice is so deep-rooted that it readily becomes the source of language play. There is a story in circulation that novelist Evelyn Waugh's agent once arranged for him to give a radio talk for a very small fee. Waugh replied to the offer:

BBC. LSD. NBG. EW.
(For younger readers, *LSD* = 'pounds, shillings, pence'.)

And then there is the game of 't'ing in i', where people try to outdo each other by talking in initials – such as *She's a v p g* ('very pretty girl'), *I've put the m in the f* ('meat in the fridge'). Sometimes initialisms are used for subterfuge. I have heard parents and dog-owners resort to the use of initial letters to avoid the human or canine listener recognizing sensitive words, such as *bedtime* or *walkies*. British lexicographer Eric Partridge found initialisms in criminal argot.[1]

There is nothing new about texting initialisms. We have both written and spoken them for years. If the above examples are not enough to convince you, start a collection of your own. It doesn't matter who you are (e.g. HRH or QC, MC or PA, VIP or OAP, IT specialist with a VG IQ) or what you're doing (sitting in your PJs drinking OJ or a G & T, in a car bought on HP doing 70 mph), there's no need to shout SOS when you see a texter writing LOL or CMB.

PS Many of these old initialisms have been adopted by texters.

PPS PTO, shortly – OK (*oll korrect*)?

Omitted letters

An initialism is a word where all the letters are omitted except the first. Often less noticeable, but certainly more common, are the cases where texters shorten words by omitting letters from the middle (often called *contractions*) or dropping a letter at the end (often called *clippings*). Usually these are vowels, in accord with information theory (p. 27), but final consonants are often dropped too, as are 'silent' consonants,

[1] Eric Partridge, *A Dictionary of the Underworld* (New York: Bonanza Books, 1949).

and double medial consonants are reduced to single-tons. There are examples of all these in the poetry in Chapter 2:

plsed	pleased	*msg*	message
bunsn brnr	bunsen burner	*txtin*	texting
messin	messing	*getn*	getting
comin	coming	*englis*	english
rite	write	*xlnt*	excellent

Other examples are *bt* ('but'), *yr* ('year'), *tmrw* ('tomorrow'), *hav* ('have'), *thn* ('then'), and *wil* ('will'). Almst any wrd cn be abbrvted in ths wy – though there is no consistency between texters, or even within a single texter. *Abbreviated* might appear in half a dozen different guises. I have seen *tonight* written as *tnight, tonyt, tonite, tonit, 2nt, 2night, 2nyt,* and *2nite*, and there are probably several more variants out there. Similar variations can be found in other kinds of electronic communication.

As with the previous features, letter omission has well-established antecedents. We only have to think of *Mr* and *Mrs* ('Mistress'), names of ranks (*Sgt, Lt*), the standard abbreviations for weights and measures (*cm, kg, ft*), or such common items as *dept* ('department'), *advt* ('advertisement'), and *asst* ('assistant'). It perhaps comes as a surprise to see that all the following text-messaging contractions can be found in

Eric Partridge's *A Dictionary of Abbreviations*, published in 1942:[2]

aftn	afternoon	*agn*	again	*amg*	among
amt	amount	*bn*	been	*btwn*	between
difclt	difficult	*evng*	evening	*fwd*	forward
gd	good	*lge*	large	*mtg*	meeting
mth	month	*togr*	together	*wd*	would

Looking through an old dictionary brings to light the interesting point that fashions in abbreviation change. Several words which were often contracted in Partridge's day no longer are. A good example is *obdt* ('obedient'), formerly common in a letter salutation ('your obedient servant'). I don't think anybody abbreviates 'opportunity' as *oppy* these days, or 'handkerchief' as *hdkf* or 'brought' as *brot*. And all of the following seem to be somewhat archaic: *clk* ('clerk'), *cml* ('commercial'), *posn* ('position' in a firm), *rcpt* ('receipt'), *rly* ('railway'), *spt* ('seaport'). It therefore seems likely that many of the current texting contractions will also disappear, as texters fall out of love with them. Probably several of those listed in the first text dictionaries have already gone. And we must expect to find new ones appearing.

---

[2] Eric Partridge, *A Dictionary of Abbreviations* (London: George Allen & Unwin, 1942).

Nonstandard spellings

Texters are also prone to mis-spell, both unconsciously and deliberately. They would not be able to use the mobile phone technology at all if they had not been taught to read and write, and this means they all had a grounding in the standard English writing system. How far they have assimilated their exposure to standard English is a moot point. Some texters will be good spellers; some will be bad. (It is the same with non-texters, as I'll discuss in Chapter 8.) But on the whole, the deviant spellings we see in text messaging give the impression of people consciously manipulating the writing system, rather than making inadvertent errors. It is worth pointing out that there are no 'spelling mistakes' in the poems and texts illustrated in Chapter 2. When the texters are not using one of the other techniques described in this chapter, they spell perfectly correctly, including some quite tricky words:

> essays, swears, wrote, better, filings, going, safely, journey, copied, receipt, postage, claim

The list of nonstandard spellings used in texting is not very great, but they are certainly distinctive – and one of the main irritants to people who do not like this genre. They include the following:

| *cos, cuz* | because | *fone* | phone | *luv* | love |
| *omigod* | oh my god | *ova* | over | *shud* | should |

skool	school	*sum*	some	*thanx*	thanks
thru	through	*wot*	what	*ya*	you

They also include representations of informal or regional speech, such as:

bin, bn	been	*da*	the
dat	that	*dunno*	don't know
gizza, gissa	give us a	*gonna*	going to
sorta	sort of	*wanna*	want to
wassup, sup	what's up	*wenja*	when do you
wiv	with	*wotcha*	what are you

But, once again, how original are they?

Several of these nonstandard spellings are so much part of English literary tradition that they have been given entries in the *Oxford English Dictionary*. *Cos* is there from 1828, *wot* from 1829, *luv* from 1898, *thanx* from 1936, and *ya* from 1941. *Wot* received a fresh lease of life at the end of the Second World War, when the watcher Chad began to peer over walls, and we learned the catch-phrase 'Wot, no —?' (the blank being filled by whatever product was in short supply). *Dunno, gonna, sorta, thru, wanna,* and *wiv* are all known from a century or more ago. Spellings such as *skool*, while not in the *OED*, are totally familiar to any reader of such comics as *Dandy* or *Beano*. It is a standard nonstandardism, as it were, thus allowing the use of *k* for *ch* to spill over into other words – such as *kemistry* (p. 15).

Many of the nonstandard spellings in text messaging can be found in literary dialect representations, such as by Charles Dickens, Mark Twain, Walter Scott, Emily Bronte, Thomas Hardy, or D. H. Lawrence. Forms like *wotcha* are in dozens of novels. Modern authors use them too. *Gissa* became well known in the UK following Alan Bleasdale's 1982 television play about a group of unemployed lads in Liverpool, *Boys from the Blackstuff* – 'Gissa job!' Other influences are commercial advertising – *Wassup* originated in a television Budweiser commercial – and pop music, especially rap lyrics, which rely heavily on nonstandard spelling. Words like *da*, *dat*, and *dis* are established representations of African-American accents. Benjamin Zephaniah starts a poem like this:[3]

> Be nice to yu turkeys dis christmas
> Cos turkeys just wanna hav fun

All long before texting was born.

Shortenings

And then, lastly, we have a kind of abbreviation where a word is shortened by omitting one of its meaningful elements, usually at the end (as in *exam*) but sometimes

[3] Benjamin Zephaniah, 'Talking turkeys', in *Talking Turkeys* (London: Puffin, 1995). <http://www.benjaminzephaniah.com/rhymin/turkey.html>

at the beginning (as in *phone*). In texting, the *day* element is regularly omitted from the days of the week (*mon, tues, sat*) as are the various month endings (*jan, feb, dec*). And the examples in Chapter 2 show further shortenings:

gran(dmother), uni(versity), bro(ther), hol(iday)s, min(utes)

This is a very natural development for this technology. Huge savings of time and money can be made if word-length can be significantly reduced without loss of intelligibility. So it is not surprising to see:

absol(utely)	ack(nowledge)	approx(imately)
arr(ive)	biog(raphy)	col(lege)
diff(erence)	doc(tor)	esp(ecially)
etc(etera)	gov(ernment)	incl(uding)
max(imum)	mob(ile)	perh(aps)
poss(ible)	prob(ably)	rad(ical)

And students naturally shorten the names of the subjects they are taking – *biol, chem, lang, lit crit*, and so on.

But none of this is novel linguistic practice. English has abbreviated words in this way ever since it began to be written down, and all of the above have long histories. Words like *exam, vet, fridge, cox*, and *bus* are so familiar that they have effectively become new words. Yet it's worth noting that when some of these abbreviated forms first came into use, they also attracted criticism. The English essayist Joseph Addison complained about the way words were being 'miserably curtailed' – he mentioned *mob(ile vulgus)*, *rep(uta-tion)*, *pos(itive)*, and *incog(nito)*. That was in 1711. And the satirist Jonathan Swift thought that abbreviating words was a 'barbarous custom'.[4] Modern texters, accordingly, find themselves part of a long tradition of criticism.

One other aspect of this kind of abbreviation needs to be noted. Apart from institutional texts (such as alerts, discussed in Chapter 6), messages are typically sent between people who know each other well. This means that the language will be intimate and local, and make assumptions about prior knowledge. It is not a criticism of texting to say that one cannot understand the following message:

did di like ham?

Both parties know who *di* is and what *ham* is (*Diane* and *Hamlet*, respectively). Any informal letter between friends would present similar difficulties of interpretation to outsiders. It is a basic principle of discourse analysis that the meaning of words cannot be grasped in isolation, but must take into account the whole situation in which the words are used. This applies as much to texting as to any other use of language.

---

[4] For the historical context, see my *The Stories of English* (London: Penguin, 2004), 303, 375.

Genuine novelties

My conclusion about the language of texting is that it is neither especially novel nor especially incomprehensible. Several of the abbreviations have been taken over wholesale from other internet activities (such as chatrooms and emails) or from earlier varieties of written language. What novelty there is lies chiefly in the way texting takes further some of the processes used in the past. From a basic *IMO* 'in my opinion' we find:

IMHO	in my humble opinion
IMCO	in my considered opinion
IMHBCO	in my humble but correct opinion
IMNSHO	in my not so humble opinion

This is a form of language play – the desire to 'up the ante' and outdo what has been done before. Traditional initialisms hardly ever did that. I shall discuss this further in Chapter 4.

Some of the juxtapositions also create forms which have little precedent, apart from in puzzles. All conceivable types of feature can be juxtaposed – sequences of shortened and full words (*hldmecls* 'hold me close'), logograms and shortened words (*2bctnd* 'to be continued'), logograms and nonstandard spellings (*cu2nite* 'see you tonight'), and so on. There are no less than four processes combined in *iowan2bwu* 'I only want to be with you' – full word + an initialism + a shortened word + two logograms + an initialism + a logogram. There are five in *ijc2sailuvu* 'I just called to say I love you' – full word + two initialisms + logogram + shortened word + full word + nonstandard spelling + logogram. And some messages contain unusual processes: in *iohis4u* 'I only have eyes for you', we see the addition of a plural ending to a logogram (cf. the 'smiles' example on p. 16).

One characteristic runs through all these examples: the letters, symbols, and words are run together, without spaces. This is certainly unusual in the history of special writing systems. In most of the examples of pre-texting language in this chapter, the abbreviated words are kept separate. Not so in texting, where some of the reported sequences of initialisms are extremely long, such as this 9-word epic:

iydkidkwd   if you don't know I don't know
             who does

As with other lengthy forms (p. 24), I doubt whether this kind of invention has any real standing in the intuitions of texters.

Graphic units of this kind are a bit like conventional words, but with the meanings of whole sentences. Like chemical formulae, they are not meant to be spoken aloud. And like all new words which don't have a clear internal structure, you have to take them as whole units. This is especially the case with ambiguous symbols. A *b*, for example, can be used either as a letter (as in *dwb* 'don't write back') or as a logogram (as in *bcame* 'became'). Similarly, we find *d8* 'date' vs. *db8* 'debate', *m8* 'mate' vs. *mbrsd* 'embarrassed', and so on. You do not know which approach to adopt until you have read the whole word. In the teaching of reading, people distinguish between 'look-and-say' and 'phonic' approaches. This is 'look-and-write' texting, rather than graphonics.

Although sequences of this kind can be found in some of the more ingenious word puzzles of the past, it is certainly a novelty to find them being used in day-to-day communication. But having said that, it must also be emphasized that they are not used all that often. Few texts string together such sequences. Texters drop the occasional one into a dialogue, and sometimes a little game arises in which groups of texters play with such sequences and try to out-text each other. But they quickly tire of the game and go back to more conventional text-messaging practices. Apart from anything else, the content of these messages is not something that turns up in dialogue very often. It might impress a potential lover to receive an initial text which said *iowan2bwu*, but the effect would quickly become counter-productive if it were sent repeatedly.

Likewise, how often in a text-messaging exchange is someone going to need to write *c u l8r* 'see you later'?

The text-messaging dictionaries are partly to blame for making people think that texting is incomprehensible. The texts in such alphabetical lists are being quoted out of context. And, moreover, out of their cultural context. If I do not understand *aslmh*, it is because I do not share a cultural milieu in which people ask each other to tell them about their 'age, sex, location, music, hobbies'. If I do not immediately grasp *prw*, it is because I no longer have to worry about whether 'parents are watching'. And in such cases as the following, whether I understand what is going on depends on how far my ear is tuned to contemporary catch-phrases:

anfscd and now for something completely different
btdt been there done that
hhoj ha, ha, only joking

Some texting expressions are exactly like slang. And 'the chief use of slang', as the old jingle goes, 'is to show that you're one of the gang'. This is where the notion of a 'code' (p. 13) has some relevance. There is no way you can 'decode' *F?* or *a3* without being a part of the group which introduced them in the first place. The first one means 'are we friends now' (after having had a row). The second is a reference to a hoped-for assignation – 'anytime, anywhere, anyplace'. Anyone not in that gang will not understand it. But that is no reason to condemn it.

It is of course possible to construct a message which deliberately juxtaposes lots of idiosyncratic or obscure usages – as in the case of the school essayist (p. 24) – but this is not typical behaviour. Any variety of language can be satirized in this way – business jargon, political speech, sports commentary, regional dialects... There is an element of truth in all parody. But it would be a travesty to believe that all members of the parodied group speak or write in that way all the time. Similarly, it is wrong to penalize all texters just because some individuals occasionally overdo it.

Individual differences there certainly are, in texting as in any other linguistic domain. While young people (and the not so young) like to feel they are part of the same gang, and show this by using the same texting abbreviations, they also like to express their individuality, and they do this by inventing new forms and using old forms in new ways. The poetry examples show this drive most clearly, but the innovation we see there can also be seen in everyday texts, which – despite the dictionary collections of textisms – are remarkably varied in spelling and style. In the absence of large surveys, it is impossible to say just how idiosyncratic a particular usage is. Of all the ways of spelling *night*, for example – *nite*, *nt*, *nyt*...– which are shared usages, which are individualistic? And, within the latter category, which are systematic and which not? In the messages of one texter, the word *you* is written *u*, *yu*, and *you* at different times. Is there any pattern here or is it random? I can imagine someone using *u* for informal or jokey messages and *you* for formal or serious ones.

Such questions can't be answered by studying single texts. Rather the notion of text dialogue has to be taken on board. We know from studies of spoken language that people influence each other in the way they speak, often by adopting features of the accent of the person they are talking to. Very likely a similar accommodation takes place in text messaging. The features I use in my text are going to be influenced by the features you use, and vice versa. If you write *u* and *nite*, then so will I. Only when I want to preserve a distance from you am I likely to reply to your *u* and *nite* by choosing different spellings, such as *you* and *night*. This of course does happen, for example in exchanges between parents and teenagers, where it would be as artificial (to the parents) and embarrassing (to the kids) for the parents to adopt teenage textisms as it would be for them to adopt teenage spoken slang, and start saying *wicked*! And I can easily imagine similar differences entering into a text dialogue when there is a cooling of a personal relationship: 'you just don't text me like you used to'.

The texting forums already provide anecdotal evidence that many texters are well aware of differences in their audience and are capable of adapting their messages to suit. Some contributors say they avoid using text abbreviations when texting parents. Some say they don't use them when texting a message to a television programme. Indeed, some channels explicitly ask for texters not to use abbreviations when sending in votes and comments. At the same time, it is clear from the websites that offer guidance about texting that many texters don't take the needs of their audience into account at all, and haven't developed a sense of appropriateness. One such site, addressing the question of vote exchanging in website competitions, begins like this:[5]

> If you vote exchange (VE) with someone, they need to know where and when they should vote for you. Most people send email daily reminders, but if it looks like the example below, your VE buddy might be totally confused.

and it goes on:

> If you use a lot of text abbreviations, some of the older generation may not understand your email at all.

The tone of these sites is not usually condemnatory. The aim is evidently to point out to texters that they have different styles at their disposal, and that they

---

[5] Spirit Tales, at <http://www.thesitefights.com/dlspec/spiritteams/countrytales/emails.html>

should make sure they choose the right one to meet the needs of their audience. This, of course, is exactly how teachers work when dealing with texting in the classroom (see Chapter 8).

Doubtless the variety of texting language is partly to be accounted for by personality differences. Some people are linguistic innovators; some are conservatives. Some people like abbreviations; some hate them (and the discussion sites are full of such words as 'hate' and 'loathe'). The same kind of antagonism can be found in relation to any area of usage, of course. When encountering a pronunciation, grammatical construction, or item of vocabulary that they do not like, people do not mince their words. Textisms are no different.

We must also expect individual differences to manifest themselves in the form of personal styles. Messages may be short, but it is nonetheless possible to draw conclusions about individual users by examining the stylistic traits that they present. Evidence for this claim comes from forensic linguistics. In 2002, Stuart Campbell was found guilty of the murder of his 15-year-old niece after his text-message alibi was shown to be a forgery. He had claimed that certain texts sent by the girl showed he was innocent. But a detailed comparison of the vocabulary and other stylistic features of his own text messages and those of his niece showed that he had written the critical messages himself. The forensic possibilities have been further explored by a team at the

University of Leicester, UK.[6] The fact that texting is a relatively unstandardized mode of communication, prone to idiosyncrasy, turns out to be an advantage in such a context, as authorship differences are likely to be more easily detectable than in writing using standard English. And it would need to be a very cunning adult indeed who would be able to replicate perfectly the distinctive texting behaviour of a teenager.

But individual differences do not explain all the variation that we find in texting. Some of it undoubtedly reflects dialect differences of a regional, social, or ethnic background. Is British and American English texting the same? I have compared texts from both sides of the Atlantic and so far found very few indications of regional difference. But there are some. Several of the nonstandard forms listed above (p. 49) plainly reflect British speech; and when a Hispanic word such as *nada* or *nd* 'nothing' turns up in an English text, the likelihood is that it is from the US.[7] Any language with an international reach will show dialect texting differences eventually. My illustrations from Spanish and Portuguese have come from Europe and South America, and

---

[6] Tim Grant and Kim Drake, Psychology Department, University of Leicester. <http://www2.le.ac.uk/ebulletin/news/press-releases/2000-2009/2006/08/nparticle.2006-08-09.0473409952>

[7] LiAnne Yu, Heilo Sacher, and Gareth Louden, 'Buddysync: pensando en los moviles para crer una aplicacion inalambrica de tercera generacion para los jovenes norteamericanos', *Revista de Estudios de Juventud* 57 (2002), 173–88. <http://www.injuve.mtas.es/injuve/contenidos.downloadatt.action?id=2040966507>

display a great deal of variation, but the samples are not large enough to be able to see whether any of the variants are regional; and asking my informants does not help, as usage is so recent that they do not have a clear intuition about what is nonstandard for their region. The issue will become clearer in due course. Text dialectology is going to be a big subject one day.

Before leaving the topic of novelty in texting, it is worth drawing attention to what happens in multilingual situations. Texters who are bilingual routinely switch between the features of their different languages. An Italian/English texter, for example, might write *2 6* for 'you are'. 'Six' is *sei* in Italian, but *sei* is also a singular form of the verb 'to be' ('you are'). The full form of 'you are' would be *tu sei*. So an English reading of *2* ('tu') has been used in order to make the text work. (In Italian, the way you say *2* is *due*.) Individual letters can also be borrowed. There is no *k* in the Italian alphabet; but when Italian texters write such words as *che* 'what', they often use *k* as a logogram, borrowed presumably from English. The English language, as we shall see in Chapter 7, is often a major influence on the way texting conventions develop in other languages.

But first, I need to deal with a question which has lurked beneath the surface of the present chapter. Why do they do it? Why has a distinctive language of texting arisen at all?

CHAPTER 4

Why do they do it?

"That's the Textas Kid — the fastest thumb in the West!"

THE PRONOUN IS `THEY´ because this question is usually asked by people who have never texted. Some, persuaded by the hype, and believing that texting is an invention of the devil, swear they never will. Some, having begun to text, swear they will never abbreviate. But eventually, most people do, for one of two reasons. It's easier. And it's fun.

Abbreviations speed things up. Sending a message on a mobile phone is – notwithstanding the virtuoso performances of many young people – not the most natural of ways to communicate. The keypad was not originally designed with language in mind: it was intended to cope with numbers, not letters. Also, many phones have clearly been designed with a focus on appearance rather than usability. Apart from anything else, phones keep getting smaller and smaller, but fingers stay the same size. So any strategy which reduces the time and awkwardness of inputting graphic symbols is bound to be attractive.

It would be easier if phones had a keypad offering the flexibility of the QWERTY keyboard, such as is found on some personal digital assistants (PDAs), BlackBerries, and the Apple iPhone. Most do not. Mobile phones typically contain only between 12 and 15 keys, and the 26-letter alphabet (for English – more for some other languages) has to be made to fit. The overloading of information on each key has led to several strategies for symbol selection, all of which are awkward and time-consuming. Here is how one system solves the problem, using a multi-press technique with a time-out. To send the sequence *def*:

- you press the '3' key: this gives you 'd'
- you wait for the time-out to complete (shown by the appearance of a flashing cursor on the screen)
- you press the '3' key twice, making sure that your second press follows the first quickly, before the time-out takes effect: this gives you 'e'
- you wait for the time-out to complete
- you press the '3' key three times, again making sure that your second and third presses follow the first quickly, before the time-out takes effect: this gives you 'f'

The sequence *def* therefore takes six key-presses plus two pauses. For punctuation marks, further key-presses would be required.

Alternatively, some phones replace the time-out with a 'next' key, which eliminates the pausing but increases the key-presses to eight, in the above example. A 'long-press' system (holding a key down for varying amounts of time) eliminates separate key-presses, but adds to pausing time. A 'two-key' method accesses every letter with just two key-presses – for example, *e* would be entered by inputting 32 (i.e. third key, second symbol) – and 'three-key' methods have been devised too. Additional strategies have to be employed, whatever the system, in order to allow choice between upper-case and lower-case letters, and to select punctuation marks and other special symbols. No system is ergonomically easy.

Nor is any system linguistically sensible. No-one took elementary letter-frequency considerations into account when designing mobile keypads. For example, key 7 on my mobile contains four symbols, *pqrs*. It takes four key-presses to access letter *s*, and yet *s* is one of the most frequently occurring letters in English. It is twice as easy to input *q*, which is one of the least frequently occurring letters. All the keys present similar inefficiencies.

Anything that reduces the problem of multiple key-presses and pauses must therefore be a good thing, and it is this desideratum which has motivated the development of *predictive texting*, where the phone uses a dictionary to guess which word you want to say. This significantly reduces the number of key-presses, but there are costs alongside benefits. An early study (2002) reported that only just over half the participants who had predictive messaging actually used it.[1] The others did not use it for a variety of reasons. Some said it slowed them down. Some missed the option to use abbreviations (though one can code them in). Some

---

[1] See Thurlow and Brown (in Chapter 2, note 3).

said their system did not offer the right words, and found the task of adding new words slow and annoying. Evidently there are still problems awaiting solution, and user comment in internet forums in 2007 seems split between those who love predictive texting and those who hate it.

The predictive approach especially increases the amount of scrolling down you have to do to find the correct word in those key-press combinations which give rise to many alternatives (what have been called *textonyms*, or *homonumeric words*), and you have to be on your mettle to avoid selecting and sending the wrong one. For example, the key-sequence 288866 gives both *autumn* and *button*; 7378378 produces both *request* and *pervert*. Some sequences generate a dozen or more alternatives. It has led to a new game: find the oddest (or most poetic) groups of textonyms. The sequence 2665, which produces both *book* and *cool*, has in fact resulted in a practice where some texters deliberately use the former word instead of the latter. 'u like the movie?' asks A. 'book', replies B.

The technology will undoubtedly develop. Alternatives to the standard keypad include touch screens, virtual keyboards, fold-away keyboards, and navigational joysticks. Text can be displayed in novel ways – for example, the Apple iPhone presents a radical alternative using speech bubbles (as seen in instant messaging) rather than linear text. The Mobile Messaging Awards, begun in 2004, have helped to focus industry attention on the areas needing improvement.[2] One of its award categories is for 'the device or software that makes mobile messaging easier'. A linguistic perspective will be essential. Perhaps a new branch of linguistic science will evolve in due course: cellinguistics. In the meantime, users have been showing their preferences in the only way they know – with their fingers, using the standard keypad.

The kind of abbreviations I reviewed in Chapter 3 began as a natural, intuitive response to a technological problem. If words could be shortened without loss of intelligibility, then this would speed the whole process up – and perhaps even save money, if the cost of a transmission were to take into account the number of symbols being sent. The remarkable thing is that nobody ever told anyone to do this. There was no ruling from the mobile phone companies which said: 'you must abbreviate'. It just happened, and in next to no time.

It happened so quickly, I believe, because texters already had an instinct about the value of shortening words in order to speed up communication, and already knew how to do it, so they simply transferred (and then embellished) what they had encountered in other settings. I pointed to many of the antecedents of texting in Chapter 3, but we do not have to go back into history to learn that, if we are in a hurry and want

2 <http://www.160characters.org/pages.php?action=view&pid=50>

to leave a written message, we are likely to abbreviate. We have all left notes in which we have replaced an *and* by an *&*, a *three* by a *3*, shortened a word-ending, and so on. It is actually one of the oldest techniques in the language. Anglo-Saxon scribes used abbreviations of this kind. In Old English manuscripts, for example, *and* was usually written with a symbol that looked like a 7. Other languages with a written history show similar strategies.

Whenever speed becomes a feature of behaviour, competitions arise. And sure enough, there are now texting competitions. In the 2007 texting championships in New York, 250 contestants competed for $25,000 in prize money. They stood with their hands behind their backs until they heard a bell and saw a message on a screen – sometimes a full-word message (such as *what we do in life echoes in eternity*), sometimes an abbreviated one (such as *OMG, nd 2 talk asap*). The first to present an accurate text version to the judges was the winner. After several rounds, the 2007 winner was 13-year-old Morgan Pozgar, who evidently trained by sending around 8,000 text messages a month to her friends.

The world's fastest texter (at the beginning of 2007), according to the *Guinness Book of Records*, was a Singaporean 16-year-old, Ang Chuang Yang. He texted the test message 'The razor-toothed piranhas of the genera Serrasalmus and Pygocentrus are the most ferocious freshwater fish in the world. In reality they seldom attack a human.' in a remarkable 43.44 seconds.

But the need to save time and energy is not by any means the whole story of texting. In fact, when we look at some text messages, they are linguistically quite complex. I have seen Japanese texts which cleverly mix letters, characters, emoticons, and other symbols, making a message which it would have been much quicker to send using conventional spelling. Some of the English abbreviations are, in their own way, quite complicated to type. So why do texters put more effort into texting than they need to? Some other factor must be involved.

This factor is the human ludic temperament. As I said above, it's fun – in the broadest sense of that word. I have elsewhere devoted a whole book (*Language Play*)[3] to exploring the extraordinary number of ways in which people play with language – creating riddles, solving crosswords, playing Scrabble, inventing new words, adopting funny accents, devising rebuses, and much more. Radio and television game shows regularly rely on language for their source material – *Catchphrase, Blankety Blank, Call My Bluff* . . . Professional writers do the same – those who provide the catchy copy for advertising slogans, those who think up the puns in newspaper headlines, those who write poems, novels,

[3] *Language Play* (London: Penguin, 1998).

and plays. It is a part of our intuition from our earliest days: something like 80 per cent of the language used to children in their first year of life is playful. And children quickly learn that one of the most enjoyable things you can do with language is to play with its sounds, words, grammar, and – later on – spelling.

The drive to be playful is still there when we text. And it is a hugely powerful drive. Even the super-pedants who condemn texting cannot resist it. John Humphrys concludes his rant against texting (p. 8) by saying 'But at least I have not succumbed to "text-speak".' Yet he ends his article with the words:

> To the editor of the OED I will simply say: For many years you've been GR8. Don't spoil it now. Tks.

A playful ending which does exactly what texters do, and for the same reason.

In *Language Play* I illustrate the extraordinary lengths to which people will go in order to play a language game. There is the famous case of *Gadsby*, the 50,000-word novel written by Ernest Wright in 1939, in which no use at all is made of the letter *e*. He must have spent months, maybe years, putting it together. And why did he do it? It is the same sort of answer as mountaineers give, when asked why they climb dangerous peaks. Because they are there. I have asked wordsmiths why they do such crazy things as write poems in which every word includes the same vowel, or every word begins with the same letter. Their answers are always the same. 'To see if I can.' Or sometimes: 'Because somebody bet me I couldn't.'

And when they get going, language players are continually 'upping the ante'. 'Write a sentence in which every word contains the same vowel'? That is not difficult. *The men were vexed.* So, make the task more difficult. Make the sentence at least ten words long. That is harder, but wordsmiths would do it quite quickly. So, make the task even more difficult. Write a whole story, of at least 200 words, with every word containing the same vowel. And, after that is done, make it harder still. Rewrite *Hamlet* with every word containing the same vowel! Now that's a real challenge. And, believe it or not, people try to do such things – and they (and eventually their readers) enjoy themselves hugely in the process.[4]

So I was not at all surprised, when I first started to examine texting in detail, to see that texters were continually 'upping the ante'. One texter would introduce an abbreviation, and another would play with it – making it longer, perhaps. Then another texter would take it further. That will be how the *ROTFL* 'rolling on the floor laughing' sequence began (p. 23) or the *IMHO* 'in my humble opinion' sequence (p. 53). Or the kind of play we see with emoticons:

---

[4] For an example of the lengths to which some people are prepared to go, see 'Hamlet: the H Quarto' at <http://www.crystalreference.com/DC_articles/Shakespeare54.pdf>.

:-)	happy
:-))	very happy
:-)))	very very happy
:-))))))	ecstatic

Homer Simpson	~(_8^(|)
Bart Simpson	3:-)
Maggie Simpson	[8-*
Lisa Simpson	{8-)
Marge Simpson	@@@@8-)

This has nothing to do with speed and efficiency of typing. This is language play.

I must admit to being taken aback by the speed with which texting developed a ludic dimension. Within two or three years of its arrival, we find the text-messaging poetry competition reported on page 13, and evidently a broad base of users very familiar with word abbreviation and keen to explore its expressive potential. The *Guardian* repeated the event in 2002.[5] Emma Passmore was the winner that year:

I left my pictur on th ground wher u walk
so that somday if th sun was jst right
& th rain didnt wash me awa
u might c me out of th corner of yr i & pic me up

[5] 2002: <http://books.guardian.co.uk/textpoetry>

And before long there were competitions all over the world. In 2003, for example, schools in Tasmania held an event for 5- to 12-year-olds.[6] This is just one out of the many entries:

> quik hurry up & txt me
> tell me u luv me
> tell me how much u want me
> tell me im da 1
> oops wrong prsn
> i sent it 2 my mum

To celebrate World Poetry Day in 2007, T-Mobile tried to find the UK's first 'Txt laureate' in a competition for the best romantic poem in SMS.[7] They had 200 entrants, and as with previous competitions the entries were a mixture of unabbreviated and abbreviated texts. The winner, Ben Ziman-Bright, wrote conventionally:

> The wet rustle of rain
> can dampen today. Your text
> buoys me above oil-rainbow puddles
> like a paper boat, so that even
> soaked to the skin
> I am grinning.

---

[6] <http://www.tasite.tas.edu.au/sms_poetry/sms_examples.htm>. There are many others, all over the world, as typing a Google search for 'text message competition' will show.

[7] <http://lovetext.typepad.com/love_text/>

The runner-up did not:

> O hart tht sorz
> My luv adorz
> He mAks me liv
> He mAks me giv
> Myslf 2 him
> As my luv porz

But what is significant about the runner-up is not so much the style as the person who produced it. No teenager, this. The author was Eileen Bridge, revealed to be a grandmother aged 68.

There have been competitions in other languages too. In 2007 a Dutch foundation created a new literary award for the most creative use of text messaging.[8] Called *De Gouden Duim* ('The Golden Thumb'), it offered prizes for messages on the themes of friendship, flirting, dumping, excuses, and art. This was the finalist in the 'excuses' category:

> b&iw! srry dak 2L8 b&: b& mt mn nwe gbrde trui
> Rgns 8ter blyvn Hkn: mst ds 1st nr Oma, om 'm te ltn mkn!
>
> DUTCH
> ben ik weer! sorry dat ik te laat ben: ben met mijn
> nieuwe gebreide trui ergens achter blijven haken.
> Moest dus eerst naar oma, om hem te laten maken.

---

[8] <http://www.onzetaal.nu/finalisten.php>

ENGLISH

Back again! Sorry I arrived too late: my newly knit
sweater got stuck behind something. So I had to go
to my grandma first, so she could fix it.

Once again, this is atypical texting. The aim is to make
the message as distinctive as possible.

The length constraint in this genre of SMS poetry
fosters economy of expression in much the same way
as other tightly constrained forms of poetry do, such as
the Japanese haiku or the Welsh englyn. To say a poem
must be written within 160 characters at first seems just
as pointless as to say that a poem must be written in
three lines of five, seven, and five syllables. But put
such a discipline into the hands of a master, and the
result can be poetic magic. Of course, SMS poetry
has some way to go before it can match the haiku
tradition; but then, haikus have had a head-start of
several hundred years.

Nonetheless, in just a few years there have been
poems that, by common consent, are highly atmos-
pheric, moving, or funny. And there is something
about the genre which has no parallel elsewhere. This
is nothing to do with the use of texting abbreviations,
which – as we have seen – are optional. Rather, it is
more to do with the way the short lines have an individual force. Peter Sansom put it like this, in his comments on the 2001 competition. Reading a text poem,

he said, is 'an urgent business...like the pools score teleprinter used to be':[9]

> having to scroll down the screen makes the reading experience entirely linear, giving real suspense to each line break, making us attend to every word and to guess ahead before the new line comes up. You can't help glancing down the page in ordinary poems for clues, for orientation; but with a text poem you stay focussed as it were in the now of each arriving line.

The impact is evident even in one-liners – poems (if we can call them that) whose effect relies on the kind of succinctness we find in a maxim or proverb. U. A. Fanthorpe loved the following submission:

> Basildon: imagine a carpark.

(There is nothing personal about Basildon here: it was one of the 'new towns' in southern Essex, UK. Any other place with a punchy sound and new, large-scale shopping facilities would have done just as well.) And both judges liked this one, with its 'in' reference to the first line of a famous poem by Philip Larkin:

> They phone you up, your mum and dad.

This is someone using a mobile phone to make a comment about mobile phones. And the same kind

---

[9] <http://technology.guardian.co.uk/online/story/0,3605,481985,00.html>

of 'self-referentiality' can be seen (in a different competition) in this SMS reworking of a famous opening line:[10]

> txt me ishmael

The rewriting of famous titles and quotations has been
a fruitful source of SMS language play in blogs, chatrooms, and forums, as it used to be with rebuses (p. 40),
as these examples show:[11]

> zen & T @ f m2 cycl mn10nc
>
> 0.5 a leag 0.5 a leag 0.5 a leag onwrd
>
> all in t valy o dth rd t 600
>
> w8ing 4 go.

The SMS genre has evident strengths, but also some
weaknesses. Its brevity disallows complex formal pat-
terning – say, of the kind we might find in a sonnet. It
isn't so easy to include more than a couple of images,
such as similes, simply because there isn't the space.
And it hardly privileges some types of writing, such as
the short story, novel, or play. Nonetheless, writers
have tried to extend the potential of the medium.

The SMS novel, for example, operates on a screen-
by-screen basis. Each screen is a 'chapter' describing

---

[10] Herman Melville's *Moby Dick*. These examples and those below come from a BBC
forum: <http://news.bbc.co.uk/1/hi/uk/2814235.stm>

[11] Zen and the Art of Motorcycle Maintenance; Tennyson: Half a league, half a league,
half a league onward / All in the valley of death rode the 600; Waiting for Godot.

an event in the story. Here is an interactive example from 2005, from a website called 'Cloakroom'.[12] The site explains the procedure:

This is the story of Rita, who carries a vital piece of information on which depends the future of India. It is written by RoGue, but controlled by you. The author keeps landing her in trouble and only you can save her. After each chapter, predict what RoGue's going to do next and upset his plans. Suggest an alternate course for the story, via comments, and fight the author.

And here is an episode from early on in the story:

Chptr 6: While Surching 4 Her Father, Rita Bumps In2 A Chaiwalla & Tea Spills On Her Blouse. She Goes Inside Da Washroom, & Da Train Halts @ A Station.

That's 152 characters, including spaces.

This is by no means the only example of its kind. In Japan, an author known as Yoshi has had a huge success with his text-messaging novel *Deep Love*. Readers sent feedback, as the story unfolded, and some of their ideas were incorporated into the story. He went on to film it at the end of the year. Then in 2004 a novel called *Out of the Fortress* by Qian Fuchang was circulated on mobile phones in China. It told a story of an extramarital affair in some 4,000

---

[12] <http://cloakroom.blogspot.com/>

words, split into sixty chapters. Since 2003, the Tokyo-based wireless service provider Bandai Networks has been offering mobile-phone books on its site: *Bunko Yomihodai* ('All You Can Read Paperbacks'). There are now around 150 titles. Readers can use their phones to write reviews and contact the authors.

The year 2004 also saw a mobile literature channel in China, sponsored by Linktone Ltd, in Shanghai. The 'm-novel', as they call it, began with a love story, *Distance*, by Xuan Huang, a well-known writer and broadcasting personality, and creator of the Taiwanese flash-media character A-Kuei. A young couple get to know each other because of a wrongly sent SMS message. The whole story is 1,008 Chinese characters, told in fifteen chapters, with one chapter sent each day. Because Chinese characters are double-byte in size, each message has only seventy characters.

Writers have explored other literary genres, such as songs, limericks, prayers, and anthems. Here is a re-writing of the British national anthem, by 'Camille, Australia'. It is, she explains, chiefly for the benefit of Microsoft Word and Outlook Express users:

Gd CTRL-S r gr8sh Qun.
Long liv r nobl Qun.
Gd CTRL-S th. Qun!
ALT-S hr vktr ES,
Hp E & glr ES,

Lng 2 rain ovR S;
Gd CTRL-S th. Qun!

And here is a rewriting of a prayer, by Matthew Campbell. It actually won a competition run by the satirical Christian online magazine, Ship of Fools:[13]

dad@hvn
urspshl
we want wot u want
&urth2b like hvn
giv us food
&4giv r sins
lyk we 4giv uvaz
don't test us!
save us!
bcos we kno ur boss
ur tuf
&ur cool 4 eva!
ok?

Plainly, there are severe limits to the expressive power of the medium, when it is restricted to a screen in this way. So it is not surprising that, very early on, we find writers – keen to explore the expressive potential of texting as a new variety of language – dispensing with

---

[13] <http://www.shipoffools.com/Cargo/Features01/Features/RFather.html>

the 160-character constraint, and engaging in SMS creative writing of any length using hard copy.

But immediately there was a problem. By taking the writing away from the mobile phone screen, how could the distinctiveness of the genre be maintained? A piece of poetry written in conventional orthography (such as the example on p. 14) would be indistinguishable from any other non-SMS poetry. So the stylistic character of SMS writing changed, when texts became longer, and texting abbreviations, previously optional, became obligatory.

Compilations of longer material are now appearing, in paper publication as well as on screen. Text-poet Norman Silver published two collections in 2006: *Laugh Out Loud :-D* and *Age, Sex, Location*.[14] Here are two extracts, to give an indication of the way he is developing the genre. His ten 'txt commandments', from the former book, are a manifesto:

1. u shall luv ur mobil fone with all ur hart
2. u & ur fone shall neva b   apart
3. u shall nt lust aftr ur neibrs fone nor thiev
4. u shall b prepard @ all times 2 tXt & 2 recv
5. u shall use LOL & othr acronyms in conversatns
6. u shall be zappy with ur ast*r*sks & exc!matns!!
7. u shall abbrevi8 & rite words like theyr sed
8. u shall nt speak 2 sum1 face2face if u cn msg em insted

---

[14] txt café, 57 Priory Street, Colchester, CO1 2QE. <http://www.txtcafe.com/>

9. u shall nt shout with capitls XEPT IN DIRE
   EMERGNCY +
10. u shall nt consult a ninglish dictnry

(The last word in the first commandment and the
capitals in the ninth are printed in red.)

My favourite from the latter book is 'langwij':

langwij
is hi-ly infectious

children
the world ova
catch it
from parence
by word of mouth

the yung
r specially vulnerable
so care
shud b taken how langwij
is spread

symptoms include acute
goo-goo
& the equally serious ga-ga

if NE child
is infected with langwij
give em
3 Tspoons of txt

b4 bedtime
& ½ a tablet of verse
after every meal

Several of the poems go well beyond text-messaging conventions, introducing line-shapes, type-size changes, font variations, colour, and special symbols which are reminiscent of the concrete poetry creations of the 1960s. They illustrate the way the genre is being shaped by the more powerful applications available on the computer.

The text-messaging novel is in print form now also. In 2007 Finnish writer Hannu Luntiala published *The Last Messages*, in which the whole 332-page narrative consists of SMS messages.[15] It tells the story of an IT-executive who resigns his job and travels the world, using text messages to keep in touch with everyone.

The growing independence of the genre from its mobile phone origins is well illustrated by the French novelist Phil Marso, who published a book in 2004 written entirely in French SMS shorthand, *Pas Sage a Taba vo SMS* – a piece of word-play intended to discourage young people from smoking.[16] In his view, reading SMS is an excellent means of learning a new language. He followed it up with a bilingual SMS oeuvre called *Frayeurs SMS* ('SMS Frights'), a collection of six short

---

[15] *Viimeiset viestit* (Helsinki: Tammi Publishers, 2007).

[16] <http://www.profsms.fr/philmarso.htm>

stories in which French is on the left-hand page and SMS on the right. Then there was *L* (2005), a retelling of French poetic classics in SMS; *la font'N j'M!* (*La Fontaine j'aime*), a retelling of La Fontaine's fables; and other works.

Marso was the brains behind 'World Without Cell Phones Day' in France in February 2000. He prides himself on never having used a mobile phone. That is the distance this new variety has travelled from the 160-character mobile screen.

CHAPTER 5

Who texts?

THE CONVENTIONAL WISDOM is that it's a teenage thing; and indeed, the surveys do show a huge bias in that direction. As early as 2002 in the UK, it was being reported that text messages had replaced phone calls as the commonest use of a mobile phone, and that the younger you are the more likely you are to text. A report in 2003 by mobile phone insurer CPP (Card Protection Plan) Group[1] said that 80 per cent of under-25s texted rather than called. On the other hand, so did 14 per cent of people over 55. Plainly, youth isn't the only factor. And in 2006, a survey by the UK regulatory body Ofcom (Office of Communications) reported that adults as a whole in the UK made on average twenty phone calls a week, but sent twenty-eight text messages.[2]

It is a global trend, which was being repeatedly seen in the early years of the new millennium. By 2002, according to the consultancy firm BDA China, 70 per cent of Chinese urban mobile subscribers had used some sort of data messaging service.[3] By 2003, in South Korea, according to Cheil Communications, 93 per cent of Koreans aged between 17 and 19 were sending or receiving a text at least once a day, with the figure reducing with age, but still a very healthy 47 per cent by age 40.[4] It would be

---

[1] <http://news.bbc.co.uk/1/hi/business/2985072.stm>

[2] *The Communications Market: Nations and Regions* (London: Ofcom, 2006), 2.1.3. <http://www.ofcom.org.uk/research/cm/nations/nations_regions/nations_regions.pdf>

[3] *Mobile subscribers in China 2002*. BDA China.

[4] Cheil Communications, *Exploring P-Generation* (Seoul, Korea, 2003).

possible to cite similar figures for several countries. The label 'thumb tribe' (*oyayubizoku*) was used for young texters in Japan, and the appellation quickly spread into China, India, and other parts of Asia.

The Norwegian researcher Richard Ling has done a great deal to clarify the age background of texters.[5] In a study reported in 2005, teens and young adults (up to the mid-20s) were, as expected, the most enthusiastic users of SMS: more than 85 per cent of this age group sent SMS messages on a daily basis. At the other end of the age scale, only 2.7 per cent of people over 67 texted daily. (I have to say that this last figure nonetheless impressed me!) Also as expected, teens and young adults were the biggest users of texting abbreviations, and there was a rapid decline of use with age. But not all features of standard English orthography showed the same pattern. Surprisingly, it was the younger adults who were *more* likely to use standard capitalization and punctuation.

Ling also found differences in texting behaviour between the sexes. Despite the fact that men were quicker to adopt mobile phones when they first became available, women turned out to be the more enthusiastic texters: over 40 per cent of women texted daily, whereas only 35 per cent of men did. In addition:

[5] 'The socio-linguistics of SMS: An analysis of SMS use by a random sample of Norwegians', in R. Ling and P. Pedersen (eds.), *Mobile Communications: Renegotiation of the Social Sphere* (London: Springer, 2005), 335–49.

- Women wrote longer messages: the mean number of words per message for women was 6.95, whereas for men it was 5.54.

- Women also wrote grammatically more complex messages: nearly 75 per cent of all messages sent by men were single-sentence texts, whereas this was 60 per cent for women. The contrast was especially noticeable in the 16-to-19-year age-group: only 48 per cent of the messages sent by girls in this group were simple; but with boys, the figure rose to 85 per cent.

- Women used abbreviations and emoticons significantly more than men (although, as we have seen, p. 22, neither group used them much).

- Women were more likely to retain the traditional conventions of orthography, using standard punctuation, capitalization, and spelling: for example, 8.5 per cent of women introduced capital letters as found in the standard language, compared with only 4.9 per cent of men.

- Women used more salutations and farewells.

- Women used texts to express a wider range of content, including far more messages with emotional content and dealing with issues of practical coordination (such as arranging to meet up).

These figures suggested to Ling that women are more 'adroit' and more 'literary' texters.

Why did it become so popular so quickly? It was partly because texting was less expensive than voice on mobiles – and in some parts of the world very much less. In China, for example, a text in 2004 cost only 0.1 RMB (roughly a US cent or half a UK penny), and for the cost of a one-minute voice call on your mobile you could send eight text messages.[6] In the Philippines, texting became the primary use of the mobile phone during the late 1990s, when the two major networks introduced free messaging – resulting in Filipino urban youth being one of the first in the world to be called 'Generation Txt'. The arrival of charging in 2000 didn't stop the development, as the costs were very low: a text cost roughly a peso, which was a twentieth of the cost of a voice call. But the charge did alter the pattern of use, with the more affluent mid-30s group becoming the most active users.[7] And even in the wealthier countries, it did not take young people long to realize the advantage of text over voice, especially when the message was being put across forcefully by mobile phone companies, and attractive payment packages were being placed in front of them.

[6] D. Turchetti, 'Teens deserve credit for hot SMS market', *21 Communications,* 28 March 2004. <http://www.21cms.com>

[7] V. Rafael, 'The cell phone and the crowd: Messianic politics in the contemporary Philippines', *Popular Culture* 15(3), 2003, 399–425; J. Toral, 'State of wireless technologies in the Philippines', in *Proceedings for Closing Gaps in the Digital Divide* (Bangkok, 2003), 173–7.

But economic factors are not the only ones, in explaining the popularity of texting. The nature of the communicating medium itself proved appealing. Among young people, in particular, texting quickly emerged as an index of belonging. Shared text behaviour shows you belong to the same 'gang' (p. 56). I do not yet know of any comparative studies, but I would expect members of a group to develop their own dialect of distinctive features, in much the same way as chatrooms do.[8] And I would also expect texting to become an index of prestige, within a group, as some members develop special kinds of expertise, such as texting speed or creative coinages. It is not just the latest model of phone which can provide kudos, but what you do with it.

Then there are the communicative strengths of the medium. Texting is far more immediate, direct, and personal than alternative methods of electronic communication. It is more convenient than instant messaging, where both sender and receiver have to be sitting at their computers. Assuming your phone is on, you are likely to receive a text message rapidly, whereas an email can sit in your inbox for a considerable time. Even if your phone is not on, the message will be stored so that you get it as soon as you turn it on. When the signal is poor, a text message can often get through when a voice message may not. This is of particular value in emergency

---

[8] See my *Language and the Internet* (Cambridge: CUP, 2nd edn 2006), chapter 5.

situations or at popular times of year when the voice phone system can be clogged: texts, using less bandwidth, stand a much better chance of getting through. Nor did it take people long to realize that there are many circumstances in which texting offers a novel opportunity for communication. In noisy environments, such as bars and night-clubs, it is a welcome alternative to speech. In the street or on public transport, it permits a level of privacy which some cultures (such as the Japanese) highly value. There turns out to be a surprising number of settings in which voice or ringtone disturbance is undesirable, such as meetings, classrooms, concerts, and libraries, and where texting allows communication to take place unobtrusively (if you have chosen 'silent' mode). In 2007, commercial trials were being conducted by Australian airline Qantas into the possible use of Inmarsat-routed SMS text messaging on their planes. The 12-month trial allowed passengers on a Boeing 767 to send text messages or emails but not voice calls, to avoid disturbing other passengers. 'Unobtrusive' is the neutral term. The value of the medium for people – old as well as young – who want to communicate secretly or subversively is also apparent.

Texting has also added another dimension to multitasking. People text while doing something else, such as watching television, listening to a lecture, attending church, and driving. Teachers have frequently observed students texting in class while reading a book, writing an essay, or even carrying out a scientific experiment. How to manage such intrusions has become an issue in itself. Some schools have banned mobile phones from their premises because of the way they are perceived to interfere with schoolwork. Following a spate of road-traffic accidents, laws to ban texting while driving are being introduced in several countries: in the US, Washington was the first state to introduce such a law (in 2007). And there have been many anecdotal reports of texting practices which conflict with traditional social expectations, such as this one from the Philippines:[9]

> Faye Siytangco, a 23-year-old airline sales representative, was not surprised when at the wake for a friend's father she saw people bowing their heads and gazing toward folded hands. But when their hands started beeping and their thumbs began to move, she realized to her astonishment that they were not, in fact, praying. 'People were actually sitting there and texting,' Siytangco said. 'Filipinos don't see it as rude anymore.'

Rude or not, such anecdotes testify to the way texting has become pervasive in many societies.

Texting also seemed to meet a new communicative need in a society where increased pressures on time and short attention spans are increasingly the norm. The

[9] <http://partners.nytimes.com/library/tech/00/07/biztech/articles/05talk.html>

medium appeals to people who do not want to waste
time engaging in the linguistic hand-shaking that is
needed in traditional face-to-face or voice telephone
conversations – what has sometimes been called 'phatic
communion' in linguistics. In those contexts it is normal
polite behaviour to exchange social messages on meeting
someone (*How are you?*, *Nice day* . . .), and in some
languages the conversational rituals of greeting and
farewell are quite elaborate. None of this is required in
texting, where the messages are typically short, direct,
and succinct, and introduced with little or no preamble.
In a face-to-face setting, they would seem abrupt or
even – depending on the relationship between the participants – rude. I received a text message from one of my
children the other day which said simply: 'Get Indie
today, good review'. It is rare indeed for conversational
interactions in English to begin so directly, without some
sort of greeting; and it is unusual even in email, instant
messaging, and other electronic conversations, where a
'Hi' or some such expression routinely breaks the ice.
Texting seems to be adding some new kinds of dialogue
to our linguistic repertoire. As one journalist put it, in
the *New York Times*:[10]

> I like text messages. They fill an ever-narrowing gap in
> modern communication tools, combining the immediacy

[10] Sandra Barron, 'R We D8ting?', *New York Times*, 24 July 2005.

of a phone call with the convenience of an answering machine message and the premeditation of e-mail. And if they happen to be from a crush and pop up late at night, they have the giddy re-readability of a note left on a pillow.

Directness has become normal and everyday in English texting. You can send me a text which gets to the point immediately, and I won't feel you have been impolite. Having seen a good number of texts from people in various parts of Europe, my impression is that speakers of several European languages feel equally comfortable in sending and receiving such messages. But we cannot generalize. The situation is undoubtedly more complicated in cultures, such as the Japanese, where conversational openings are traditionally more leisurely and negotiated in character. Someone who adopts a direct style, in these cultures, runs a risk of contravening indigenous norms of politeness and respect. Many young people, influenced by Western texting style, are now doing just that, and attracting criticism from older people as a consequence. How far these new styles will be influential in altering the character of speech acts in these languages remains to be seen.

The climate has to be right, though, for texting to take off. Not everywhere took up texting at the same time. The most noticeable contrast was between the US and Europe, especially the UK. I remember introducing the topic of text messaging to a group of teachers in New York in 1999, describing the British trends, and finding to my surprise that none of my audience had any experience of it, nor did they know of any students who used it. The US began to catch up five years later. But why was there a lag at all?

There is a cluster of reasons, according to American linguist Naomi Baron.[11] She argues that personal computers became a routine part of homes and schools much earlier in the US than in most other countries. American youngsters thus had a great deal more typing experience using conventional keyboards. In some junior schools, indeed, students often do almost all their written work on computer. As a result, alternative methods, such as email and instant messaging, became very popular, and there was little motivation to learn a new (and more awkward) set of typing skills.

She also draws attention to economic circumstances. Landline phones including voicemail have been a routine and relatively inexpensive part of US culture for some time. Talk, as they say, is cheap. Subscription plans offer thousands of 'free minutes'. There was thus less motivation to use a phone to text when telephonic voice communication was so much a part of

---

[11] Naomi Baron, personal communication, September 2003; but see also N. Baron and R. Ling, 'IM and SMS: a linguistic companion', International Conference of the Association of Internet Researchers 4, October 2003.

your regular way of life. Also, if you have more private space (your own room, your own phone), the need to text is less of an imperative. And cost is not such a big issue in the US among teenagers and college students, because most mobile phone bills are paid for by parents.

In addition, the slow start in the US was to a considerable extent the result of different technologies and standards being used by different telecommunications companies across the country. Many of the handsets in the US market were not equipped to send SMS messages until 2001. And it was only in early 2002 that SMS became generally interoperable between most of the US wireless telecoms. Before that, the US scene, as one commentator put it, was 'a crazy-paving of licenses covering the country'.[12]

And Baron makes a very interesting social point. Texting is not so easy in a land where driving is so much a part of everyday life; and this difficulty has increased now that states are beginning to make it illegal to text and drive. By contrast, in countries where people rely more on public transportation (and spend a great deal of time waiting for it to arrive), texting has a real social and time-filling function.

But the benefits of texting, it seems, have made the medium irresistible. A 2007 report from the US-based

---

[12] Jon Agar, *Constant Touch: a Global History of the Mobile Phone* (Cambridge: Icon Books, 2003).

CTIA – the International Association for the Wireless Industry – records that 158 billion text messages were sent in the USA in 2006, a 95 per cent increase over the previous year. It concludes: 'America is in the midst of text messaging mania'.[13]

[13] <http://www.ctia.org/consumer_info/safety/index.cfm/AID/10672>

CHAPTER 6

What do they text about?

WHAT ARE PEOPLE TALKING ABOUT when they send text messages to each other? This sounds like an easy question to answer, but it is in fact very difficult, because texting data is very difficult to get hold of. Would you let me see the messages you send and receive? I have asked many people, and most give me a knee-jerk negative reaction. I had already encountered resistance when collecting email and chatroom data for my *Language and the Internet*, but people were far more reluctant to let me see their texts. It was as if I had asked them for a window into their most intimate world.

There is an additional problem over the messages you receive. It wouldn't be ethical for me to use those messages without obtaining the permission of the senders, and how is *that* to be arranged? Moreover, if I am doing some work on the age, gender, and social background of texters, how am I to get hold of such information? I would have to ask you to interrogate your senders about these things – and that in itself is a time-consuming and possibly sensitive business. It is easy to see how texters might be reluctant to cooperate with researchers, once they realize the problems.

Then there are the practical problems. Do you keep a copy of the messages you send and receive? Even if your phone has plenty of storage space, the ephemeral content of most messages makes it unlikely that you will keep them for long. And even if you do, how can I, as a researcher, get at them without causing you unacceptable levels of interference? If I ask you to transcribe them for me, will you do this honestly (without filtering out some intimate or risqué details) and will you be able to do it accurately? Will you be sure to keep the messages exactly as they are, with all their abbreviations and errors? And if, to avoid these problems, I asked you to set up some sort of auto-forwarding system to my computer, would you be happy for this to happen, so that I see everything? And finally, even if these problems are solved, will I be able to understand the messages you give me? They will, after all, be part of an exchange with someone about subject-matter to which I am not privy (p. 52).

Nonetheless, researchers have been able to make useful collections of texting data between individuals, where even a small corpus of a few hundred messages can demonstrate interesting linguistic patterns. For example, Richard Ling's study, referred to on page 90, confirmed several impressions about the linguistic character of text messages:

- Their brevity: if we divide messages into those containing a single sentence or clause ('simple'), and those containing more than one ('complex'), we find that two-thirds of all text messages are simple.

- Their nonstandard orthography: around 82 per cent of all messages had no capitalization at all; 11 per cent had only the first letter of the text capitalized;

and only 7 per cent had more complex capitalization (e.g. using capitals in names and at the beginning of follow-up sentences).

- Their distinct epistolary status: only about 10 per cent of messages had an opening salutation (e.g. *Hi, John, J*) or a closing farewell (e.g. *Bye, xxx, Dave*), and most of these were the simplest possible, such as a single letter or an emoticon.

- Their lack of abbreviations: only about 6 per cent used abbreviated forms of any kind, regardless of age and gender.

Plainly, if most texts are single sentences, and the average length is around six words (p. 91), the routine content of text messages must be pretty limited, concentrating on everyday and largely ephemeral notions of who, what, where, and when (rather than on more profound and long-lasting explorations of how and why). But within this limitation, texts perform a wide range of social and informational functions.

Social functions

All kinds of social relationships can be fostered or disturbed using texting, from the mildest of observations to the strongest of affirmations. People can send messages of support, sympathy, variants on 'missing you', variants on 'get well soon', a request for a call, a desire to be friends ... It can be a message reflecting the time of day – a good morning or a good night. It can be a quotation or other remark which simply affirms a shared interest. Exchanging personal news and gossip is as important here as anywhere else. Greetings, such as for a birthday or a religious feastday, are ideally suited to the brevity of a text message. Some industry surveys suggest that as many as a quarter of all text messages fall into this category. Incidence varies with time of year. On New Year's Day in 2007, a new record was set for daily text messages in the UK: 214 million.

By no means all social messages are positive. The system is just as able to send insults, put-downs, accusations, and libels, and a great deal of concern has been expressed about the way texting has been used as a mechanism of bullying among young people. Several cases of text-stalking and harassment have been reported. And at least one study, by Bella Elwood-Clayton, has reported how texting can be used as 'a form of artillery in personal combats'.[1] Many of her Philippines informants commented on how easy it was to quarrel by text.

Slowly, as a need becomes apparent, help becomes available. An interesting development was reported in 2006 by the Samaritans, who had spent some years looking into young people's use of texting. They

[1] Bella Elwood-Clayton, 'Desire and loathing in the cyber Philippines', in R. Harper, L. Palen, and A. Taylor (eds.), *The Inside Text: Social, Cultural and Design Perspectives in SMS* (Dordrecht: Springer, 2005), 197.

found that 94 per cent of 18- to 24-year-olds sent personal text messages, and these were beginning to come through to their centres. Their official statement gave one illustration:[2]

> Feel so down n don't know who 2 turn 2. Don't think
> I cn cope anymore cos things at home are realy getin
> 2 me. Plz help cos I don't know what 2 do.

Their volunteers are now ready to receive messages by text and are trained to respond to them in the same way. The official statement went on:

> Volunteers have received training in the reading of
> 'abbreviated text language' but all replies from
> Samaritans will be in full spelling, except for when
> using small or clearly recognised abbreviations.

And one of the volunteers is quoted as saying:

> I had thought that text messaging would be an
> impoverished version of email. It isn't. It is closer to a
> phone call with more interactions than email. It goes at
> a slower pace than a phone call but it is a rich medium
> that gives us a new way of interacting with callers.

Text messaging has a huge potential for offering help and advice. Parents in particular are gradually coming

---

[2] <http://www.samaritans.org/know/pressoffice/news/2006/news_250406_popup.shtm>

to realize that texting can actually help them in their role, if they adopt it. An American survey carried out for Mediathink in 2006 found that 63 per cent of parents who text believed that it improved their communication with their child.[3] A similar comment is made below from Japan. And several new ideas have been implemented. For example, 2006 saw the launch in the USA of the PRMTXT Campaign, for parents concerned about their teenagers getting drunk at a student prom (the formal high-school or college dance, held towards the end of an academic year). They visit www.prmtxt.org to register their child's cell-phone number, the date of the prom, and their zip code. On the prom night, the teen receives a message: 'Have fun 2night. Stay safe. Don't drink. Luv u.' The message can be customized with the name of a particular person. It is one of several texting initiatives being promulgated by CTIA, the US-based International Association for the Wireless Industry.[4]

Quite a few messages, especially among young people, engage in grooming, flirting, or their converse, as they enter into relationships or break them. The popularity of this category is illustrated by the many texting abbreviations which swear undying love. A text message is also, according to several online forums, the

---

[3] <http://www.textually.org/textually/archives/2006/08/013379.htm>

[4] <http://www.ctia.org/content/index.cfm/AID/10664>

easiest and least embarrassing way to tell someone that you no longer want to go out with them. Texting evidently allows an intimate person-to-person contact while preserving distance. 'You can say some things in text that you can't say face to face' is a common observation in forums about texting.[5]

Observations of texting behaviour, such as this one from Japan, arc typical:[6]

At a busy hamburger restaurant in Fukuoka, I observed *keitai* dating [keitai = 'mobile' in Japanese], or *go-kon*, a mysterious ritual whose intricacies had to be explained by my Japanese hostess. Four boys and four girls were facing each other across a table. Talking was confined to whispered messages delivered boy to boy and girl to girl. Under the table (which I couldn't see), everyone was furiously typing on their *keitais*, showing messages to their neighbors. The closest direct girl/boy contact occurred at the end of the evening, a shy exchange of phone numbers. Other *keitai* social rituals are documented in '*Keitai* Log', a web diary published online by a group of college students researching the role of *keitai* in Japanese society. A recent diarist observed that *Keitai* culture actually strengthens ties

[5] For example, at this magazine website: <http://www.mkeonline.com/story.asp?id=343910>

[6] Lucy Haagen, 'You go girl, Japanese style', *Community Technology Review*, Winter 2004–5. <http://www.comtechreview.org/winter-2004-2005/000230.html>

between parents and children. She reported that GPS systems are now standard *keitai* features, and that many high school girls relieve academic stress by text-messaging their mothers during the long school day.

A great deal of social texting is motivated by boredom. If one has nothing much to do, then one might as well send a text – and at any time of the day – or night. (Around 20 per cent of teens say that they send and receive SMS messages after midnight on a weekly basis.) It is a handy way of killing time. In one study of schoolchildren, Timo Kopomaa draws an interesting analogy with children's play:[7]

> Composing text messages in all kinds of places is akin to the tendency, found in children's play, to move away from inactivity towards activity. The text message transports the sender's thoughts to the recipient, offering the sender the freedom from the constraints of the immediate environment: the aim is escape. However, escape in this case is primarily based on the contact established with the recipient rather than a wish to get away from one's physical setting.

The desire to play, as I argued in Chapter 4, is a dominant influence on texting as a genre, so it is not surprising to see text messages which are exclusively devoted to ludic activities, being used to circulate jokes, riddles, clever remarks,

---

[7] Timo Kopomaa, 'The breakthrough of text messaging in Finland', in R. Harper, L. Palen, and A. Taylor (see note 1), 150–1.

and chain messages. Timo Kopomaa found that 65 per cent of text messages in his study were sent for fun rather than for a serious purpose. Many websites have been devoted to SMS jokes, in a variety of languages, with the jokes broken down into dozens of categories – marriage, politics, animals, sex – as on any joke site. The limited size of the screen privileges jokes that are one-liners or quickfire dialogues, and the effect is at times not dissimilar to the rapid give-and-take of music-hall repartee. Unlike most other text messages, a word-play message does not require a response; rather, the recipient is expected to pass it on.

Some countries have gone in for ludic texting in a big way. The leading providers of subscription-based text messages in China (Sina, Sohu, Netease) hire teams of SMS authors (*duanxin xieshou*) to write funny or entertaining texts – including jokes, clever greetings and farewells (the number of variants on how to send a good-night kiss is breathtaking), hoaxes, quotes, erotica, and trivia.[8]

Informational functions

One of the most noticed functions of texting is its role in helping people plan their lives, coordinating times,

---

[8] See the account by Long Chen, 'I am a backstage manipulator of SMS culture' (wojiushi duanxinwenhua de muhouheishou), Guangzhou: *New Weekly* (*xinzhoukan*), Guangzhou, 15 July 2002, p. 39. A typical selection of English ludic texts can be found at <http://www.txtmania.com/messages/text.php>.

arranging or cancelling a meeting, ensuring that arrangements go smoothly, checking on the whereabouts of someone or something, and so on. In Guadeloupe, a colloquialism for the mobile phone is actually *le t'es où* ('the where are you?'). A remarkable number of perfectly ordinary, daily, family activities are now organized in this way, especially in relation to travelling and redirection of journeys. Not all coordination is lawful: texts have been used in the planning of fraud, terrorism, and other illegal activities.

Messages often ask questions and provide responses to do with specific points of information. Especially popular are enquiries about the results of sports events. The category is increasing with the growth of television programmes which invite viewers to text a vote or response to something they have just been watching. In two-way interactive text messaging, enquiries can be sent to a search engine, which then sends a response (often in a sequence of text pages) to your mobile phone. Here too there can be an 'illegal' side, such as receiving help from outsiders in a quiz or exam.

All kinds of organizations now send out text messages alerting users who are on their mailing list to the latest news from their domain. It might be news about weather conditions, travel conditions, sporting fixtures, school timetable changes, a 'thought for the day'... Broadcasting companies, such as the BBC, CNN, and Sky, offer a News SMS alerts service. Users register their mobile number with the service, and details of major national and international events are sent as they happen. Some local government authorities (such as Liverpool and Sheffield) have begun to alert subscribers to all kinds of events in their area – floods, traffic holdups, terrorist incidents, planning decisions, rubbish collections ... In the aftermath of the Virginia Tech shootings in April 2007, when email alerts proved so unsatisfactory as a means of warning students of danger, universities began to explore the possibilities offered by texting.

Some countries, such as China and The Netherlands, have been experimenting with texting 'neighbourhood watch' schemes, in which the police use SMS to alert local people to a missing child, a spate of burglaries, and so on. In the USA, a campaign began in May 2006 called 'Wireless Amber Alerts', designed to help increase the number of people who might be able to help in locating an abducted child. It is a development of the Amber Alert system (Amber being the first name of an abducted child found murdered in 1996), which has been in place since 1998. When news of an abduction reaches the police, they issue an amber alert, sending a message to the National Center for Missing and Exploited Children. The information in this alert is then formatted and sent out via the various service providers to text message subscribers.[9]

---

[9] <https://www.wirelessamberalerts.org/index.jsp>

A great deal of mobile commerce and banking now relies on text messaging, as does advertising and branding for the marketing industry. Several organizations send out regular SMS newsletters. There are a number of specific applications. For example, in 2005 Master-Card launched a service in which registered customers receive a text message whenever a suspicious transaction has been made, cutting response times by the company by as much as 90 per cent. And in a stock market application, you can do such things as configure the alert system to text you when a particular stock falls below a certain price.

A commonly used metaphor, especially in the context of 'alerts', is to talk about the technology facilitating the 'push' of information. Information is being pushed out to recipients as it becomes available. The contrast is with a 'pull' model, where people poll a server regularly to see if any new information is there. The pull model is obviously wasteful of time, energy, and bandwidth, for most of the time there will be little or no change in the data source. Far better, for many purposes, is to ask to receive only that information which is relevant to your needs and to know that it will arrive at the earliest possible moment. At the same time, it costs the user to receive each message, so services have to tread a fine line between under-sending and over-sending. And a push model is only efficient if you have a clear and narrowly defined focus on the kind of information you want.

Developments in the use of texting are taking place all the time. In one range of applications, your mobile can be linked with others to allow a text-based multi-party interaction, in the manner of a chatroom. Another range includes email, fax, or voicemail notification systems. With email, for example, a server sends a text message to your mobile phone whenever an email arrives in your inbox. The message can include information about the sender, the sender's e-address, and even the opening of the message. You can also customize the procedure so that you get alerted only if the message comes from a particular sender or contains particular keywords.

A third example of a novel application is the use of a 'validity period'. Imagine you are about to watch an hour-long TV programme, and you want to text friends to tell them it's on. You send a text, but you have no way of knowing if your friends' phones are on or not. If they are, your message will reach them. But if they aren't, your message is of value only if they turn their phone on in the next hour. If they turn on their phone two hours later, your message is not only useless; it might also be annoying. However, if you set the validity period of your message to 'one hour', the SMS server will not forward your message once the deadline has passed. A new interpretation of the old maxim, 'What the eye doesn't see . . .'.

Another television development is the emergence of SMS-to-TV chat, which seems to have started in

Finland in 2001. Viewers sent messages to a phone number, and these were displayed on TV – after passing before the eyes of a moderator, who monitored message content – in the manner of rolling news headlines. The idea caught on, with some participants texting frequently (despite the cost involved in sending messages), interacting just as they would in a chatroom. Not surprisingly, the idea soon added a game-show dimension, with messages controlling events on screen. Whether this kind of enterprise will spread remains to be seen. In 2004 a new Finnish channel, VIISI, began broadcasting, totally devoted to interactive TV, but it lasted only for a few months.

Text chat has even become art. In 2006, German artist Matthias Haase created an SMS chat sculpture, 'Der Bote' ('The Messenger'), at the University of Fine Art in Dresden.[10] It consisted of a steel table holding a computer, screen, and projector, with a GSM module to receive text messages. Visitors could send a message from their phone to the number shown on the screen, and these would be broadcast a few seconds later; the system then sent a brief reply from the author. Once news of the installation travelled, messages came in from all over the world.

As people become more aware of the communicative potential of texting, the range of specialized uses

---

[10] A picture can be seen at: <http://openpr.com/news/2569.html>.

grows. In politics, for example, text messaging has been repeatedly found as a good way of bringing an issue to the attention of party members, activists, or even larger sections of the population. In 2007 it was reported that the Home Office was using SMS to reach foreigners in the UK whose visas were about to expire. In Nigeria, it was used to monitor the state of affairs at the polls in the 2007 presidential elections. And text messages have reached people who would otherwise be unaware of events. The huge attendance at the demonstrations which followed the Madrid train bombings in 2004 was largely facilitated by thousands of text messages which ended with *pasalo* 'pass it on'. If you wanted to receive regional updates during the 2004 presidential campaign of Howard Dean, an early front-runner for the Democratic nomination, you could sign up to receive two texts a month. Hillary Clinton did the same in 2007. And election campaigns in Korea, Kenya, and the Philippines have all been influenced by texting. Communications commentator Howard Rheingold observes:[11]

> The electoral power of texting could be an early
> indicator of future social upheaval: whenever people
> gain the power to organize collective action on new
> scales, in new places, at new tempos, with groups

[11] 'Political texting: SMS and elections': <http://www.thefeaturearchives.com/topic/ Culture/Political_Texting_SMS_and_Elections.html>

they had not been able to organize before, societies and civilizations change.

Text messaging is also a convenient way of organizing the ephemeral events known as 'flash mobbing', where a crowd of people gather in a public place at a predetermined time to participate in a (usually pointless) stunt.

The influence of text messages in marketing campaigns is also being explored. One team, at the Clinical Trials Research Unit in Auckland, investigated the use of text messaging as an aid to giving up smoking.[12] They sent out texts to 850 young smokers (average age 25), such as 'Write down 4 people who will get a kick outta u kicking butt. Your mum, dad, m8s?' The smokers received five messages a day for a week before their designated 'quit day' and for the following four weeks. Then they received three messages a week for a further five months. As an incentive, they were also given one month of free personal texting, starting on their quit day. Another group of young smokers received a month of free texting six months after their designated quit day, but no text messages designed to help them quit. Six weeks after quit day, 28 per cent of the group that received the texts claimed to have quit, compared with 13 per cent of the control group.

[12] A. Rodgers, T. Corbett, D. Bramley, T. Riddell, M. Wills, R.-B. Lin, and M. Jones, 'Do u smoke after txt? Results of a randomised trial of smoking cessation using mobile phone text messaging', *Tobacco Control* 14 (2005), 255–61.

The researchers thought that several factors could be involved. Apart from the encouragement that the text messages provided, they felt that the extra texting opportunities given to the test group had a part to play. As recipients of texts, the arrival of messages on a variety of topics could have provided a useful distraction from the urge to smoke. And as senders, the task of texting might have had a similar function, giving smokers something else to do. At one point the researchers describe texting as 'chewing gum for the fingers'.

From the illustrations in Chapters 5 and 6, it is easy to see that text messaging is a worldwide phenomenon. The mobile phone companies have a global reach, and people everywhere seem to text with similar motivations. The one major point of difference is that they text in different languages. Hitherto, my examples of usage have been restricted to English. It is time now to see whether what holds for English also holds for other languages.

CHAPTER 7

How do other languages do it?

T HE SHORT ANSWER IS: in more or less the same way as English does (Chapter 3), at least for those languages which use the Roman alphabet. As far as I know. If it is difficult for an English-language researcher to get hold of reliable data for English (p. 103), it is very much more difficult to obtain it for other languages. In collecting material for this chapter, I was reliant on the good will of friends and family abroad and the occasional discovery of a website where someone has been thoughtful enough to report some of the texting conventions they use in their own language. There is no international corpus of texting conventions, yet.[1]

What this means is that the examples in this chapter (and in the Appendix word-lists) must be taken only as illustrations of the kind of thing that goes on in these languages. All I can say with confidence is that each example had at least one genuine use in someone's text message. I do not know how frequent the illustrated forms are, or whether they occur in alternative spellings (though when I have seen these, I have added them). Undoubtedly, many variants of these forms occur in a language. Particularly unclear is whether

[1] But a large corpus of (Belgian) French SMS exists: C. Fairon and S. Paumier, 'A translated corpus of 30,000 French SMS': <http://cental.fltr.ucl.ac.be/pub/2006-Fairon-Paumier-SMS-LREC.pdf>. See also Jacques Anis, *Parlez-vous texto? Guide des nouveaux langages du réseau* (Paris: Le Cherche Midi, 2001). A special issue of *Revista de Estudios de Juventud* (Madrid: Instituto de la Juventud) reviewed SMS usage in several countries: *Juventud y telefonos moviles* (No 57, June 2002), <http://www.injuve.mtas.es/injuve/contenidos.item.action?id=149095362&menuId=1969776808>. See Appendix B for websites containing SMS abbreviations in languages other than English.

there are preferences for upper-case vs. lower-case forms. On the whole, people prefer lower-case, partly to avoid the extra key-push required to introduce capitalization, but also because of the general avoidance of capitals in internet communication, where they are perceived as SHOUTING. I have used therefore lower-case variants throughout (including German, where one would normally expect to see initial capitals for nouns and some pronouns).

Because the examples are limited and serendipitous, they will sometimes give a false impression of difference. If I illustrate abbreviation X in language A and not in language B, this doesn't mean that X does not occur in language B. It simply means that I haven't seen an example of X in language B.

Most of the material I have found is for languages which use the Roman alphabet – reflecting the bias towards that alphabet which has been a familiar story in relation to the development of the internet as a whole. Indeed, we might go further and say the bias towards the *English* alphabet, for that was the dominant language of the internet in its early years, and it is very noticeable how shoddily the less familiar (to English eyes) accented characters of languages that use Roman script have been treated on web-pages – generally omitted or replaced by their unaccented equivalents. This bias is evident in texting too. The Czech alphabet, for example, contains the letters č, ě, š, and ž.

These diacritics are almost always omitted in Czech text messages, so that the letters appear as *c*, *e*, *s,* and *z*. The context is usually sufficiently clear to ensure that ambiguity is avoided. Similarly, the tilde in Portuguese is often replaced by an *m*, as in *entaum* for *então* 'then' and *naum* for *não* 'not'.

When we consider the huge differences in structure and writing system among the 6,000 or so languages of the world, it is plain that those which come to be used in texting will need to adapt themselves to the technology in very different ways. It is already interesting to see how non-Roman writing systems, such as those using logographic characters or symbols based on syllables, are finding ways of making the keypad work to handle their language's individuality. The scale of the problem can be seen in languages such as Ethiopian, where the writing system contains 345 symbols. In Arabic texts, numerals can be used to replace letters that don't exist in the Roman alphabet; for example, a *2* is used to show an Arabic glottal stop, so that *insha'llah* 'God willing' appears as *insha2llah* (though usually abbreviated to *isa*).

How does one make the keypad cope in the case of a language with complex characters, such as Chinese? Three solutions are currently available. One method uses a multi-key-press system. The first key-press enters a basic character or character-element, and further key-presses enter additions and variations. The process is guided by the way Chinese is normally written. The strokes which make up a character belong to a small number of groups, and they are drawn in a specific order. These groups are linked to locations on the mobile phone, so, by pressing the keys in the order in which the strokes would be drawn on paper, it is possible to build up the required character.

Another method makes use of an alternative writing system, such as the widely used phonetic system known as *pin-yin*, which writes Chinese words down using letters of the Roman alphabet. The name *Beijing*, for example, contains two characters, one written as *bei* and the other as *jing*. To obtain the first character, texters press the letters *b*, *e*, and *i*, and this brings up several candidate characters, all of which are pronounced 'bei'. They choose the character needed for the first syllable of *Beijing*, and then proceed to the second syllable, pressing *j*, *i*, *n*, and *g*. Another set of candidate characters appears, and they choose the relevant one.[2]

A third method, available on really smart phones, is to rely on handwriting recognition. One writes the character onto the mobile phone screen, and the software converts it into the text-messaging equivalent. This may well be the future, but the approach is still

---

[2] For an example of this process in action, using zhu-yin spelling, see Yuan-Ting Erica Huang (2007), 'Mobile phone keypad design for fast Chinese text entry by phonetic spelling': <http://www.acm.org/src/subpages/huang/SRCGrandFinal_EricaHuang.html>.

in its infancy, and presents the familiar problems (e.g. errors due to sloppy handwriting) facing all systems of automatic writing recognition.

Problematic also are languages where the average word length is greater than in English. Many languages of the world have very long words (they are technically called 'agglutinative' languages) and many have a rich system of inflections (word-endings which change meaning, such as the plural -*s* ending for nouns in English). English has very few inflections, and few long words in everyday use. The average number of letters per word in English is about five. (There are 2,744 letters and 581 words in my Preface, for example – an average of 4.7.) By contrast, in Malayalam, one of the languages of India, the average word-length is closer to 10; in Inuit (Eskimo) it is about 14. Both these languages contain hundreds of inflections. Texting abbreviations, such as omitting vowels, might help a little, in such cases, but they do not provide a total solution (even if everyone were inclined to use them) because so much meaning is expressed in the inflections by the vowels.

The temptation to abbreviate must be just as strong for a Malayalam or Inuit who starts to text as it is for a texter in English or Italian. And as a texting culture develops in a particular language, it is very likely that different preferences will emerge and novel kinds of abbreviatory conventions appear. For example, in Tagalog (Philippines), repeated syllables, often used to build up verb forms, are avoided by using a numeral: for example, *mamaya* 'later' can be written *ma2ya*. Some languages, indeed, may well find the transition to texting a smoother process than in English, because their writing system is already naturally abbreviated. A writing system which does not represent vowels, or represents them indirectly (as in Semitic languages), is already doing something which English texters consider unusual.

Or consider the case of languages whose writing system is strongly phonetic: that is, a regular one-to-one relationship exists between sounds and letters – something which is strikingly lacking in English. Texters in these languages are unlikely to go in for rebuses of the *c u r* type (p. 40). It is precisely because English has such unpredictable spellings as *see*, *you*, and *are* that abbreviating to *c*, *u*, and *r* has a point. In a language where this kind of irregularity does not exist, the option is simply not available. That is presumably why one does not find this kind of texting convention in Czech, for example – apart from in words which have been borrowed from English.

English does tend to complicate things, in the study of multilingual texting, because it is frequently encountered in languages where texters are using their mother-tongue to write their messages. I have omitted English textisms from the lists in my Appendix B, so I should therefore mention here that text messaging in every language I have observed makes use of abbreviations borrowed from English ('loan texts'), or introduces forms which show English influence. For example, *lol* ('laughing out loud') is found everywhere, as are *U* ('you'), *brb* ('be right back'), and *gr8* ('great'). The acronym *SMS* seems to have been borrowed wholesale, and *thx / thanx* and *ily / ilu* 'I love you' turn up in several languages replacing the home-grown phrases. Sometimes the Anglicism affects just part of the native word, as in Dutch *2m* ('tomorrow', though the Dutch word is *morgen*) and *2d* ('today', for *vandaag*).

Some texters pepper their messages with 'cool' English expressions. Here is a sample of English loans which I have seen used in German texting, with the standard equivalent in parentheses:

b4   before (*bevor*)
4u   for you (*für dich*)
4e   for ever (*für immer*)
brb be right back (*bin gleich wieder da*)
j4f just for fun (*nur zum spaß*)
mx   Merry Christmas (*Frohe Weihnachten*)

I have seen *now* used in place of *maintenant* in French – which is certainly a time-saver! There may even be abbreviations used frequently which do not turn up in English texting, or which are used there very rarely – in much the same way as loan words from English are sometimes used in ways that are not actually English, as in French *le parking* 'the car park'. In Chinese texting, for example, one encounters the abbreviation *ft* for *faint*, meaning 'ridiculous'.

Not surprisingly, texts are found which conflate two languages (what in linguistics is referred to as *code-mixing*). This is a German example:

> *mbsseg*   mail back so schnell es geht ('as fast as you can')

And these are Russian ones, neither using abbreviations:[3]

> *forvardni mne soobschenie* ('forward me a message')
> *replui mne bistro* ('reply to me quickly')

As most parts of the world are bilingual, I would expect code-mixing to develop to be a major characteristic of texting; but we will need larger samples of data before this can be demonstrated.

Why has English had such an influence? There are several reasons. It is partly because of the language's status as a global lingua franca. English is a desirable language for international communication, so it is hardly surprising to see its use when people text, if English learning has been part of their language background. There is a natural tendency for languages to borrow words from other languages, and the use of English as a source for new words has been one of the most striking trends in recent decades. A second reason is that the UK

---

[3] Olga Vershinskaya, 'Comunicacion movil como fenomeno social: la experiencia Rusa', *Revista de Estudios de Juventud,* 57 (2002), 139–49. See URL at note 1.

was quick to adopt the technology, so it has had longer for its texting conventions to evolve and spread. And a third reason is that texters in other languages had already been exposed to many so-called textisms through their experience of English language chatrooms, where abbreviations such as *lol* and *brb* had long been in use.

One consequence of the influence of English is that it seems to have cramped the creative style of young texters in their own languages. Repeatedly, when I asked people to send me examples of their language's textspeak I would be told that they do not have very much because everyone prefers to use the English conventions. This turned out not to be entirely true, as the following examples show, but there is no doubt that the code-mixing of English and native textisms is a major feature of the international texting scene.

In the case of European languages, the crosslinguistic parallels in the use of texting conventions are striking. If we take each of the abbreviation types illustrated for English in Chapter 3, we can find analogous usages in other languages. The same innovative processes seem to be at work everywhere.

Pictograms and logograms

Some symbols are so universally used that their logographic presence in text messaging is virtually guaranteed. Whatever the word for 'and' is, the symbol & is likely to be found; and the same principle applies to the numerals and the use of the @ sign. The way these symbols are pronounced then controls their distribution in words as syllable replacements, as in the case of *2day* and *4ever* (p. 38). Thus we find:

Italian *sei* 'six' used for *sei* 'you are'
example: *dv 6* = *dove sei* ('where are you')
German *acht* 'eight'
example: *gn8* = *gute Nacht* ('good night')
Spanish *dos* 'two'
example: *sl2* = *saludos* ('greetings')
French *sept* 'seven', pronounced 'set'
example: *k7* = *cassette* ('cassette');
Welsh *un* 'one'
example *1ig* = *unig* ('only')
Russian *пять* 'five', pronounced 'pyat'
example: *o5* = *опять* 'again' ('opyat')
Swedish *ett* 'one'
example: *d1a* = *detta* 'this'
Norwegian *sy* 'seven'
example: *7k* = *sjuk* 'sick'
Czech *pět* 'five'
example: *z5* = *zpět* 'back'
Persian *do* 'two'
example: *2nya* = *donya* 'world'
Hungarian *egy* 'one'
example: *1ik* = *egyik* 'either'

In Bulgarian, we find just the initial letter of numerals motivating the use of a logogram. For example, 'four' is 'chetiri' (in the Cyrillic alphabet, четири) and 'six' is 'shest' (шест), but Bulgarian SMS (in the Roman alphabet) uses such forms as *4akai* = *chakai* 'wait' and *ka6ti* = *kashti* 'home'.

Numeral sequences also occur. In French we find *koi29* = *quoi de neuf* 'what's new' – where *de* 'of' = *deux* 'two' = *2* and *neuf* 'new' = *neuf* 'nine' = *9*. French also provides a nice example of a group of three: *a12c4* = *à un de ces quatres* 'see you around' (literally: 'to one of these fours').

How many numerals are likely to be used in this way depends primarily on their length as pronounced words. Most numerals are short, often monosyllabic, and are thus easily substituted for syllables in longer words. A longer numeral, such as *4* in French (*quatre*), Italian (*quattro*), and Spanish (*cuatro*), is unlikely to be much used, because the sound sequence it represents is infrequently encountered in longer words in those languages.

Welsh is a language which readily illustrates texting use of most of the numerals. I have found no examples of *4* (*pedwar*) or *6* (*chwech*), though they are theoretically possible in a few words such as *pedwarawd* and *chwechawd* ('quartet' and 'sextet' respectively – presumably *4awd* and *6awd*). But all the other textisms are found on a Welsh texting site – though this does not mean that they are frequently used. (And indeed, some of the words in the table are unlikely candidates for text messages!)

Welsh numerical textisms

No	Welsh	Pronounced	Txt	Welsh word	Pronounced	Meaning
1	un	'een'	blod1	blodyn	blod-in	'flower'
2	dau	'die'	blo2	blodau	blo-die	'flowers'
3	tri	'tree'	3st	trist	treest	'sad'
5	pump	'pimp'	5io	pwmpio	poomp-yo	'pump' (verb)
7	saith	sigh-th	7u	saethu	sighth-ee	'shoot'
8	wyth	oo-ith	8nos	wythnos	with-noss	'week'
9	naw	now	9r	nawr	nowr	'now'
10	deg	day-g	braw10	brawddeg	brow-theyg	'sentence'

Welsh texting also brings to light an interesting usage: *9*, on its own, for the Welsh colloquial word for 'grandmother', *nain*. Here we see the influence on texting of a bilingual culture. The English pronunciation of *9* is being used to represent a Welsh word which happens to have the same sounds. The Welsh pronunciation is irrelevant here, for that (see the table) is *naw*.

Another example is in the use of @. The Welsh word for 'at' varies: depending on the idiom, it might be translated as *yn*, *ger*, or in other ways. But when the syllable *at* appears in a Welsh word it is often texted using the @ symbol with its English pronunciation. We thus find such forms as @F *ataf* 'to me', @CH *atoch* 'to you', and @B *ateb* 'answer'.

As with other texting conventions, this kind of inter-linguistic pun is not new. Generations of schoolchildren were taught Latin and thereby encountered such word-play as *Caesar adsum jam forte – Antonius sed passus sum*. This is nonsense in Latin, but makes sense when the syllables are interpreted as if they were English: 'Caesar had some jam for tea – Antonius said pass us some'. Other languages offered comical definitions, such as French *pas du tout* 'father of twins' and *entrechat* 'let the cat in'. It is an old kind of bilingual language play (technically called 'macaronic language' – from *macaroni*). Bilingual texting has hit upon the same process– taking a word from one language and giving it a meaning from another. In this case we are talking about a logo-gram rather than a word, but the principle is the same.

All the examples that I have seen show the influence of English. Welsh *ciw* is represented by *Q* (though there is no letter *q* in the Welsh alphabet). Japanese texting uses the logogram pair *39*. The word for 3 is *san*, and for 9 is *kyu*. Combined, we get *san-kyu*, and this is used as an abbreviation for 'thank-you'. *3Q* is used in Chinese on a similar basis (the pinyin for *3* is *san*). And a mixture of Japanese and English appears in this more complex example, 0840:

0 = *oh*, as in the English numeral

8 = *ha*, a shortened form of Japanese *hachi* 'eight'

4 = *yo*, a shortened form of Japanese *yon* 'four'

0 = *oh*, as in the English numeral

The combination produces *ohayoo*, 'good morning'. Other coinages using the same principle are 0833 *oya sumi* 'good night' and 724106 *nani shiteru* 'What are you doing?'

The use of numerals in Japanese texting has its antecedents. In the 1990s, Japanese girls devised number-strings as codes for the pagers (*pokeberu* – 'pocket bells') which were so fashionable at the time. Today, the same kind of inventiveness is seen in SMS *gyaru-moji* ('girl-talk'), which is a mixture of Japanese syllables, numerals, emoticons, and other characters.[4] English has its presence there too.

The use of a numeral to represent a character with the same or similar sound is also well established in Chinese. For example, *7456* would be given the following representation in the pinyin alphabet:

   qi   si   wu   liu

These forms are then used to represent the Chinese characters pronounced:

---

[4] Kenichi Fujimoto, 'The third stage paradigm: territory machines from the girls' pager revolution to mobile aesthetics', in Mizuko Ito, Daisuke Okabe, and Misa Matsuda (eds.), *Personal, Portable, Pedestrian: Mobile Phones in Japanese Life* (Cambridge, Mass: MIT, 2005).

qi   si   wo   le

which are interpreted as:

annoy   dead   me   past tense marker

A free translation of this would be 'It was really annoying' – or perhaps, more colloquially, 'You pissed me off'. Some lengthy inventions have been observed in the ludic language of lovers, such as *8807701314520*, literally translated as 'Hug hug you, kiss kiss you, whole life whole life I love you'.

An interesting complication in Chinese, which awaits detailed study, is the way the various Chinese languages (which use the same written characters) sound out these characters differently, thus making it more likely that a symbol will be used in one language rather than another. For example, the character for 'eight' is pronounced /pa/ in Mandarin and /pa:t/ in Cantonese. The character for 'not' is /pu/ in Mandarin and /pat/ in Cantonese. The phonetic relationship between 'eight' and 'not' is clearly much closer in Cantonese, making it more likely that a possible message such as 02825 ('Do you love me or not') will be used and unambiguously interpreted.

Also interesting in Chinese is the way numeral logograms and characters combine. For example, the combination

8错

means 'not bad', using the *8* once again to stand for 'not'. Some combinations of this kind mix English and Chinese. For example:

4人民

means 'for the people'. And *B4* illustrates a further possibility for English/Chinese mixing, for this can be read in two ways. Given a wholly English reading, it is 'before'. But in Chinese, the pinyin reading of *4* is *si*, and the combination *bi-si* is close to *bi-shi*, which means 'despise' – so *B4* can also be seen with that meaning in Chinese texting.

Sometimes the influence of one language upon another is seen in the spelling. Polish texters often use English *sh* instead of their native *sz* or *ż*. There is no *x* in the Czech alphabet, but it will be seen in texts as a substitute for k + s:

> *jak se máš?* 'how are you?' becomes *jaxe mas*
> *pak se uvidíme* 'see you later' becomes *paxe uvidíme*

In Italian texting, we might see the alien letters *j*, *k*, or *y*. *K* is especially popular, for it is used to replace *ch* or *c* in many common words:

ke che 'what'		*anke anche* 'also'	
ki chi 'who'		*qlk qualche* 'some, any'	
ks cosa 'thing'		*qlks qualcosa* 'something, anything'	

km come 'how'   *qlk1   qualcuno* 'someone, anyone'

The same thing happens in other Romance languages where *qu* is common, such as Portuguese *pekena* = *pequena* 'little' and French *keske* = *qu'est-ce que* 'what'. Similarly, there is no *x* or *v* in Welsh, but we nonetheless find such abbreviations as *bxo* for *bec-sio* 'worry' and *v* for *fi* 'me' (*f* is pronounced as an English *v*).

Single-letter logograms tend to be language-specific, often reflecting the pronunciation of the letter-name or symbol in the language's alphabet. In French texting, for example, *g* is regularly used for *j'ai* 'I have' because that is how the name of the letter *g* is pronounced ('zhay'). The useful phonetic value of *t* ('tay') in French is also apparent from these examples:

gt   *j'étais* 'I was'
tt   *t'étais* 'you were'

In Italian, the multiplication operator *x* is pronounced *per*, so this symbol is used to replace *per* in texts, whether as a separate word (meaning 'for') or as a syllable:

x te	*per te* 'for you'
xh	*per ora* 'for the time being'
sxo	*spero* 'I hope'
xché, xké, xk	*perché* 'why, because'
xò	*però* 'but'

xsona	*persona* 'person'

A similar thing happens in Spanish: $x = por$ 'for', $xfa = por\,favor$ 'please', $xq = porque$ 'why, because'.

These French examples show an unusual use of an obligatory capital letter:

l's tomB	*laisse tomber* 'forget it'
je le saV	*je le savais* 'I knew it'

The capitals are used as reminders to pronounce their letter-names in full – French *B* is pronounced 'bay' and *V* as 'vay'. By pronouncing the letters in this way, *tomber* is correctly read as 'tom-bay' and *savais* as 'sa-vay'. If the words had been abbreviated with lower-case letters, as *tomb* and *sav*, they would look as if they were shortened words; and while there is no reason for French texters not to use such forms, it is interesting that the phonetic value of the letters has in these cases 'outranked' their graphic value.

Italian and Spanish are also languages in which texters use the plus and minus signs quite a lot. The plus sign is often there to represent the 'superlative' ending, *-issimo* – as in Italian *mmt+*, which stands for *mi manchi tantissimo* 'I miss you so much'. An example of the latter can be seen in Italian *−male*, which stands for *meno male* 'less bad', i.e. 'luckily'. This also happens in Portuguese: + for *mais* 'more' and − for *menos* 'less', with + − for *mais ou menos* 'more or less'. In Spanish the use of + for *más* 'more' then gets used in such words as +*tikr* for *masticar* 'chew'. In Hungarian, + is used for *meg* 'more', and thus in such words as +*y* for *megy* 'go'. These practices are unusual in English – I have found a plus sign only in *t*+, 'think positive' and in the occasional formula, such as *u*+*me* 'you and me'. I haven't (yet) seen a minus sign used logographically in an English text message.

Initialisms, omissions, and shortenings

All the languages I have investigated use the other abbreviatory processes described in Chapter 3. The reduction of words to their initial letters is seen in these examples:

Italian	*tvb*	*ti voglio bene* 'I like you a lot'
Spanish	*tq*	*te quiero* 'I love you'
French	*stp*	*si'l te plait* 'please'
Polish	*zw*	*zaraz wracam* 'be right back'
Japanese	*w*	*warau* 'laughing'
Arabic	*d*	*di* 'this'
Tagalog	*k*	*ka* 'you'
Hungarian	*szvsz*	*szerény véleményem szerint* 'IMHO' (= in my humble opinion)

It is notable that German texters, influenced by the convention in the standard language, often capitalize the initial letter of nouns; but there is great variation.

And indeed, in lists of German SMS words, initialisms are the most common form of abbreviation, as this longer selection (shown here with their capitalization) illustrates:

BS	*bis später* 'see you later'
dad	*denk an dich* 'thinking of you'
dg	*dumm gelaufen* 'shit happens!'
DiV	*Danke im Voraus* 'thanks in advance'
Ff	*Fortsetzung folgt* 'to be continued'
G	*Grinsen* 'grin'
HDOS	*Halt die Ohren steif* 'keep a stiff upper lip'
KA	*Keine Ahnung* 'no idea'
khzm	*kommste heut zu mir* 'come out with me today'
KK	*Kein Kommentar* 'no comment'
MWN	*Meines Wissens nicht* 'not to my knowledge
Pg	*Pech gehabt* 'bad luck'
ssz	*schreib schnell zurück* 'write back quickly'
sTn	*schönen Tag noch* 'have a good one!'
ts	*träume süss* 'sweet dreams'
UAwg	*Um Antwort wird gebeten* 'RSVP'
www	*wir werden warten* 'we'll wait'

Combinations of initials and logograms are seen in these German examples:

G&K	*Gruß und Kuss* 'love and kisses'
3n	*nie, niemals, nirgendwo* 'no way, no how, nowhere'

The latter has a parallel in English *A3* 'any time, any place, anywhere'.

By contrast, initialisms are relatively unusual in Welsh abbreviations. One of the few examples I've found is *gtw* (= *gweld ti wedyn* 'see you later'); another is *tiv* (= *ti i fi* 'you to me'). Part of the reason may be that Welsh is a language in which the initial letters of words traditionally mutate, depending on the grammatical context. For example, the noun *pen* 'head' becomes *ben* after the word for 'his', *phen* after the word for 'her', and *mhen* after the word for 'my'. The word *fi* 'me' in *ti i fi* is an example: it is a mutated form of *mi*. The risk of texting ambiguity is apparent, if the initial letter of a word could be any of three letters. But mutation cannot be the only reason, as these variant forms are disappearing from modern informal Welsh.

All the languages shorten words by using combinations of initial and medial letters:

Spanish	*tb*	*también* 'also'
Italian	*trp*	*troppo* 'too much'
German	*aws*	*auf wiedersehen* 'good-bye'
Portuguese	*msm*	*mesmo* 'same'
Chinese	gg	*gege* 'brother'

And several use combinations of initial, medial, and final or penultimate letters.

Tagalog	*bka*	*baka* 'maybe'

Portuguese   *bjs*   *beijos* 'kisses'

The samples are small, but it is possible to sense certain trends. In French and Spanish we often see abbreviations ending in a word's final consonant:

French
bcp   *beaucoup* 'very much'
pr   *pour* 'for'
tjs   *toujours* 'always'

Spanish
dcir   *decir* 'say'
fvor   *favor* 'please'
mjr   *mejor* 'better'

But this is unusual in Italian, where there is a tendency to avoid having abbreviations end in a vowel, so that we find many examples like:

sl   *solo* 'alone, only'
spr   *sapere* 'know'
cmq   *comunque* 'anyway, however'
smpr *sempre* 'always'
qnd   *quando* 'when'

Spanish texters, by contrast, seem to have no objection to vowels ending a text abbreviation:

nka   *nunca* 'never'
qndo *cuando* 'when' (note the *q* in place of *cu*)
kro   *caro* 'dear'

cia   *compañía* 'company'

However, they do avoid a vowel with certain types of word-ending, such as *-ante / -ente*:

bstnt	*bastante* 'enough'
exclnt	*excelente* 'excellent'
gralmnt	*generalmente* 'generally'
gnt	*gente* 'people'

Another idiosyncrasy is that Spanish texters use double letters to express plurals for time periods:

aa	*años* 'years'
dd	*días* 'days'
mm	*meses* 'months'

We sometimes find just medial letters used:

Dutch	*ff*	*effen* 'even'
Welsh	*lla*	*efallai* 'perhaps' (*ll* is a single letter)

Most of the above examples can't easily be spoken because of their lack of vowels. German, however, shows a different pattern in such examples as the following, where the shortened syllables make pronounceable words:

lamito	*lache mich tot* 'laughing myself to death'
sofa	*Sonntagsfahrer* 'Sunday driver'
bihoba	*bis hoffentlich bald* 'see you soon, hopefully'
tabu	*Tausend Bussis* '1000 kisses'

Longer abbreviations make use of combinations of all the above processes, often ingeniously constructed, as in German *zumiozudi?* = *Zu mir oder zu dir?* 'My place or yours?' Some have to be carefully deconstructed, as with French *g1id2kdo* = *J'ai une idée de cadeau* 'I have a great idea':

g = letter-name pronounced 'zhay'

1 = numeral name = *une*

i = letter-name pronounced 'ee'

d = letter-name pronounced 'day'

2 = numeral name pronounced 'deux' = 'de'

k = letter-name pronounced 'ka'

do = phonetic pronunciation as 'doh'

These examples illustrate the kind of thing that goes on when people in different languages text each other. The same set of abbreviatory processes described for English in Chapter 3 seems to be in use everywhere, with just a few variations reflecting the properties of the individual languages, and messages illustrate the same range of functions. Having said that, cultural differences are bound to exist. For example, a 2005 study by Carole Anne Rivière and Christian Licoppe showed that there is a marked contrast in behaviour between texters in Japan and France.[5] In Japan, people

---

[5] Carole Anne Rivière and Christian Licoppe, 'From voice to text: continuity and change in the use of mobile phones in France and Japan', in R. Harper, L. Palen, and A. Taylor (eds.), *The Inside Text: Social, Cultural and Design Perspectives in SMS* (Dordrecht: Springer, 2005), 103–26.

find text valuable as a means of maintaining social propriety, avoiding the embarrassment and potential loss of face which can accompany an unwanted face-to-face interaction or phone call. They also see texting as a way of avoiding the constraints of formal codes of expression: many of the markers of respect ('honorifics') that are a part of the normal spoken language are omitted in text messages. These factors are far less important in France, where texts are seen as a way of managing privacy in a public space, allowing communication while maintaining a silent presence. When they wish to express emotion, or be playful, Japanese texters make more use of emoticons and other pictograms; French texters rely more on written language, abbreviated or full, and make more use of word-play. We need many more studies of this kind.

Faced with a new kind of communication problem, presented by mobile phone technology, people all over the world have set about solving it in the same kind of way. They have done so, not by inventing a new language, but by adapting old language to suit the new medium. It is not the first time people have adapted language to meet the needs of new technological circumstances. The arrival of printing, wireless telegraphy, telephony, broadcasting, and the internet all pulled language and languages in fresh directions, introducing new standards and styles. Each set of innovations took years to evolve, and was influenced primarily by adult experts, such as printers, engineers, and broadcasters. But texting is different. Here we have a set of linguistic adaptations being introduced by youngsters, on their own, spontaneously, rapidly, and without professional tuition. I have, quite frankly, never seen anything like it.

Nor, of course, had anyone else. Which is presumably why so many people panicked when they first encountered it.

CHAPTER 8

Why all the fuss?

A REMARKABLE NUMBER OF doom-laden proph-ecies arose during the opening years of the new millennium, all relating to the linguistic evils which would be unleashed by texting. The prophecies went something like this:

- Texting uses new and nonstandard orthography.
- This will inevitably erode children's ability to spell, punctuate, and capitalize correctly – an ability already thought to be poor.
- They will inevitably transfer these new habits into the rest of their schoolwork.
- This will inevitably give them poorer marks in examinations.
- A new generation of adults will inevitably grow up unable to write proper English.
- Eventually the language as a whole will inevitably decline.

There was never any clear evidence supporting these assertions, but that did not stop them being made. And when someone found a piece of writing which did seem to support the argument – the child who sup-posedly wrote her essay entirely in a texting style (p. 24) – it was immediately publicized as being typical of a generation. The one extract from that essay was reproduced in hundreds of newspapers and websites all over the world. The full essay, if it existed, was never presented. And no other examples of this kind have since been found. Every time I talk to groups of teachers and examiners, I ask them whether they have encountered anything remotely similar. None of them ever has.

In 2007 I had the opportunity to work with some groups of teenagers studying for A-levels at various schools in the UK. They all texted. I asked them whether they would use text abbreviations in their schoolwork. They looked at me with blank incomprehension. One said, 'Why would you ever want to do that?' They were perfectly clear in their minds that texting was for mobile phones and not for other purposes. 'You'd have to be pretty stupid not to see the difference', said another. The point was affirmed many times in a BBC forum which followed the report on the child's essay in 2003, such as this comment from 11-year-old Charlotte:[1]

> I write all my notes in txt, like from a video, if I were
> going 2 do an essay on it (which I do in normal
> language), but I wouldn't do it for proper work,
> ESPECIALLY IN EXAMS.

Or this one from 15-year-old Terri:

> I have never heard of anyone using 'text language' for
> an essay or anything, and if I did, I'd probably hurt them
> horribly. But, it's not my problem if you get horrendous

---

[1] <http://news.bbc.co.uk/cbbcnews/hi/chat/your_comments/newsid_2814000/2814357.stm>

grades for something ridiculously stupid you did if you
happen to use it. I don't understand how people can't
tell the difference between what CAN be used in English
(which is correct English, duh) and what can't, like text
language or whatever.

Doubtless there are some children who can't 'tell the
difference', and who therefore introduce the occasional
text spelling or abbreviation into their written work.
Teachers and examiners have told me of cases, and
I have seen some examples of work in which a few
abbreviations appear. But the instances were few and
sporadic, evidence of carelessness or lack of thought
rather than a systematic inability to spell and punctuate.
I also got the impression, from the general appearance of
the handwriting, that some of the writers were simply in
a hurry, and in their rush to get ideas down and complete a paper in time used some abbreviations in much
the same way as anyone might replace *for example* by
e.g. or use an *etc.* to replace some items in a list.

The formal examination reports are not much help,
for they present an unclear picture, and their conclusions
are distorted by media hype. For example, in 2006, the
chief examiner's report of the Irish State Examination
Commission drew attention to a concern over one section of the Junior Certificate:[2]

[2] <http://www.examinations.ie/archive/examiners_reports/cer_2006/JC_English_2006.
pdf>

Expertise in text messaging and email in particular would appear to have affected spelling and punctuation. Text messaging, with its use of phonetic spelling and little or no punctuation, seems to pose a threat to traditional conventions in writing.

The comment was made in relation to the 'Personal Writing' section of the examination; no similar comments were made in relation to the other six sections of the exam. The conclusion in the second sentence – even allowing for its cautious phrasing – hardly seems warranted, therefore. But it takes very little to rouse the prophets of doom.[3] And not surprisingly it was the 'threat' which motivated all the headlines, in which the language of possibility was transformed into the language of definite fact:

> Shock: text messages blamed for declining standards in written language (*Mobile Digest*)
> Text messages destroying our language (*The Daily Opinion*: see p. 7 above)

Also in 2006, the Scottish Qualifications Authority commented that text abbreviations were appearing, but only in a 'very small' percentage of exam papers.[4] In relation

---

[3] For an excellent collection of media quotations along these lines, see the paper by Thurlow referred to in Chapter 1 (note 8).

[4] <http://www.sqa.org.uk/files_ccc/CourseReportEnglish2006.pdf>
<http://www.sqa.org.uk/files_ccc/PAReportEnglishStandardGrade2006.pdf>

to the task of 'Folio Writing', they comment on things that some candidates found 'demanding':

> observance of the conventions of written expression and, in a few cases, the avoidance of the inappropriate use of the informalities of talk and, occasionally, 'text language'

It was a comment made for the Standard Grade only, not for the Intermediate 1 and 2, Higher, or Advanced Higher. Note the qualifications: 'few cases', 'occasionally'. This was not enough to stop adverse political reaction and media comment about the language being 'murdered' (to take a headline from *The Sunday Times*).[5]

Tim Shortis, a former chief examiner for English language A-level at the exam board AQAB, said he had rarely seen textisms used in A-level papers, though they were more common at GCSE level. He commented:[6]

> There's a moral panic about young people and language, a populist alarm. But the examples you see in the media are rarely used. You get initialisms such as *LOL* for 'laugh out loud' and letter and number homophones such as *r* and *2*, but they are not as widespread as you think. There are also remarkably few casual misspellings.

[5] Katie Grant, 'Our language is being murdered', *The Sunday Times*, 5 November 2006. <http://www.timesonline.co.uk/tol/newspapers/sunday_times/scotland/article624235.ece>

[6] <http://www.tes.co.uk/search/story/?story_id=2341958>

It would be strange if it were otherwise. As we have seen in earlier chapters, very few words in a language are abbreviated by texters – we are talking about a few dozen common words and phrases, and certainly not hundreds. Not all young texters use the abbreviated forms. And those who do use them do not use them very much – in as few as 6 per cent of messages, in the Norwegian study reported earlier (p. 90). People who talk of texting as a 'new language', implying that the whole of the writing system is altered, are inculcating a myth.

None of this is to doubt the frequently reported observation that there are many instances of poor written work in schools. But it is crucial to recognize the various causes of inadequate literacy. There are indeed children who are weak at writing, poor spellers, and bad punctuators. There always have been. Possibly up to 10 per cent of the child population have learning difficulties (such as dyslexia) in which reading and writing are specifically affected. The problems facing these children are increasingly being recognized. But there is nothing new about them. They were there long before texting was invented.

Another group of children are said to be poor writers and spellers, compared with previous generations, for a whole host of other reasons – too much television, too many video games, too much internet, not enough reading . . . It is not my purpose in this book to explore these issues. All I want to point out is that these reasons pre-date texting. The claim that there has been a decline in writing skills, whatever its merits, goes back decades. It is the theme of the opening pages of the Bullock Report on English.[7] That was in 1975. This report quoted several firms complaining about the poor levels of spoken and written English in their employees. One firm said that they were having 'great difficulty in obtaining junior clerks who can speak and write English clearly and correctly, especially those aged from 15 to 16 years'. That was in 1921.

I do not see how texting could be a significant factor when discussing children who have real problems with literacy. If you have difficulty with reading and writing, you are hardly going to be predisposed to use a technology which demands sophisticated abilities in reading and writing. And if you do start to text, I would expect the additional experience of writing to be a help, rather than a hindrance.

There is a curious ambivalence around. Complaints are made about children's poor literacy, and then, when a technology arrives that provides fresh and motivating opportunities to read and write, such as email, chat, blogging, and texting, complaints are made about that. The problems associated with the new medium – such as new abbreviation styles – are highlighted and the potential benefits ignored. I heard someone recently

[7] *A Language for Life* (London: HMSO, 1975).

complaining that 'children don't keep diaries any more'. The speaker was evidently unaware of the fact that the online diary – the blog – is one of the most popular areas of internet activity among young people.

A couple of axioms might be usefully affirmed at this point. I believe that any form of writing exercise is good for you. I also believe that any form of tuition which helps develop your awareness of the different properties, styles, and effects of writing is good for you. It helps you become a better reader, more sensitive to nuance, and a better writer, more sensitive to audience. Texting language is no different from other innovative forms of written expression that have emerged in the past. It is a type of language whose communicative strengths and weaknesses need to be appreciated. If it were to take its place alongside other kinds of writing in school curricula, students would soon develop a strong sense of when it is appropriate to use it and when it is not. It is not as if the school would be teaching them something totally new. As I illustrated at the end of Chapter 3, many websites are already making texters aware that there are some situations in which it is inappropriate to use texting abbreviations, because they might not be understood.

This might seem to be self-evident, yet when a text-messaging unit was included as an option in the English curriculum in schools in Victoria, Australia, for students in years 8 to 10, it was condemned by no less a person than the federal minister of education.[8] The students were being taught to translate SMS texts, write glossaries of abbreviations, and compare the language of texting with that of formal written English. Stylistic comparisons of this kind have long proved their worth in English classes; their value is repeatedly asserted in the documents which led to the UK English National Curriculum, for example, and the comparative study of standard and nonstandard varieties of language is now a regular event in the English classroom – and not only in the UK.[9] The minister was reported as urging a return to 'basics'. But what could be more basic, in terms of language acquisition, than to focus on students' developing sense of linguistic appropriateness?

The knee-jerk antagonism to texting as a variety of language is fostered by the misinformation about it in the media. For example, on 9 November 2006 Wikipedia accepted an entry which was headed 'New Zealand students able to use txt language in exams'.[10] It began:

The New Zealand Qualifications Authority (NZQA) has announced that a shorter version of English known

---

[8] <http://www.abc.net.au/worldtoday/content/2006/s1760068.htm>

[9] For example, in the Kingman Report (London: HMSO, 1988), section 4.29, and many other places.

[10] <http://en.wikinews.org/wiki/New_Zealand_students_able_to_use_txt_language_in_exams>

as txt language will be acceptable in the external end of year exams.

This seems absolutely clear-cut, and if it were true – given the widespread suspicion of texting – likely to provoke an outcry. But the NZQA site the next day told a very different story:[11]

> The Qualifications Authority is actively discouraging candidates in NCEA exams from using abbreviations, including text-style abbreviations. Deputy Chief Executive, Qualifications, Bali Haque said there had been no change in the Authority's policy in regard to use of abbreviations in examinations. Where an examination requires candidates to demonstrate language use – i.e. sentence structure, grammar, spelling – they would be penalised for using abbreviations, Mr Haque said . . . [because] use of abbreviations creates a risk of answers not being understood.

Far more people find the Wikipedia site than the NZQA one, of course, so the error lives on.

Misinformation of this kind can be crushed only by solid research findings. And research is slowly beginning to show that texting actually benefits literacy skills. The studies are few, with small numbers of

---

[11] <http://www.nzqa.govt.nz/news/releases/2006/101106.html>

children, so we must be cautious; but a picture is emerging that texting does not harm writing ability and may even help it. Here are the findings of some recent studies:

- Veenal Raval, a speech and language therapist working at the City University in London, compared a group of 11- to 12-year-old texters with a similar group of non-texters.[12] She found that neither group had noticeably worse spelling or grammar than the other, but that both groups made some errors. She also noted that text abbreviations did not appear in their written work.

- A team of Finnish researchers found that the informal style of texting was an important motivating factor, especially among teenage boys, and provided fresh opportunities for linguistic creativity.[13]

- In a series of studies carried out in 2006–7, Beverly Plester, Clare Wood, and others from Coventry University found strong positive links between the use of text language and the skills underlying success in standard English in a group of pre-teenage

---

[12] <http://www.city.ac.uk/marketing/dps/Citynews/email_bulletin/0060%20Citynews%20email%20bulletin%20-%2010%20January%202005.pdf>

[13] E.-L. Kasesniemi and P. Rautiainen (2002), 'Mobile culture of children and teenagers in Finland', in J. E. Katz and M. Aakhus (eds.), *Perpetual Contact: Mobile Communication, Private Talk and Public Performance* (Cambridge: Cambridge University Press), 170–92.

children.[14] The children were asked to compose text
messages that they might write in a particular
situation – such as texting a friend to say that they
had missed their bus and they were going to be late.
The more text abbreviations they used in their
messages, the higher they scored on tests of reading
and vocabulary. The children who were better
at spelling and writing used the most texting
abbreviations. Also interesting was the finding
that the younger the children received their first phone,
the higher their scores.

These results surprise some people. But why should
one be surprised? Children could not be good at texting if they had not already developed considerable
literacy awareness. Before you can write abbreviated
forms effectively and play with them, you need to have
a sense of how the sounds of your language relate to
the letters. You need to know that there are such things
as alternative spellings. You need to have a good visual
memory and good motor skills. If you are aware that
your texting behaviour is different, you must have
already intuited that there is such a thing as a standard.
If you are using such abbreviations as *lol* ('laughing

[14] Beverly Plester, Clare Wood, and Victoria Bell (2008), 'Txt msg n school literacy: does mobile phone use adversely affect children's attainment?' *Literacy* 42, 137–44 and Beverly Plester, Clare Wood, and Puja Joshi (2009), 'Exploring the relationship between children's knowledge of text message abbreviations and school literacy outcomes', *British Journal of Developmental Psychology* 27, 145–61.

out loud') and *brb* ('be right back'), you must have developed a sensitivity to the communicative needs of your textees, because these forms show you are responding to them. If you are using *imho* ('in my humble opinion') or *afaik* ('as far as I know'), you must be aware of the possible effect your choice of language might have on them, because these forms show you are self-critical. Teenage texters are not stu pid nor are they socially inept within their peer group. They know exactly what they are doing.

What teenagers are not good at is fully understanding the consequences of what they are doing, in the eyes of society as a whole. And this is where teaching (in the broadest sense of the word) comes in. They need to know when it would be appropriate to text and when it would not be. They need to know when textisms are effective and when they are not. They need to appreciate the range of social reactions which texting, in its various forms, can elicit. This knowledge is slowly acquired from parents, peers, text etiquette websites, and (in the narrow sense) teachers. Teenagers have to learn to manage this new behaviour, as indeed do we all. For one thing is certain: texting is not going to go away, in the foreseeable future.

These arguments are not unique to texting. They apply equally to the other 'literacies' which children need to acquire if they are to achieve a fluent command of their language as readers and writers. Here are three sentences from the previous paragraph, but with the texting terminology replaced by terms relating to a different variety of language:

> They need to know when it would be appropriate to use scientific language and when it would not be. They need to know when scientific jargon is effective and when it is not. They need to appreciate the range of social reactions which scientific jargon, in its various forms, can elicit.

You could replace 'scientific language' by many other terms: 'literary language', 'poetic language', 'journalistic language', 'advertising language', 'nonstandard language', 'regional dialect'... The aim of language education is to put all these literacies under the confident control of the student, so that when they leave school they are able to cope with the linguistic demands made upon them.

Texting is just another variety of language, which has arisen as a result of a particular technology. It takes its place alongside the other mediums of electronic communication which have resulted from the internet revolution. Texting is not alone, and many of its linguistic properties are shared by other kinds of computer-mediated communication. For example, text messages are short; but so are several other forms of electronic expression. In fact they are not the most succinct form: that record is held by instant messaging. A comparative study by Richard Ling and Naomi Baron showed that almost 60 per cent of text messages contained more than one sentence while only 34 per cent of instant messages did.[15] Sentences were longer in texting and there were more characters per message. Texts are more autonomous. This is unsurprising: it would be awkward and uneconomical to continue a lengthy chat dialogue by mobile phone. Because each text message has an individual cost, messages tend to be fuller and more self-contained. Instant messaging, by contrast, readily spreads the content of a message serially over several transmissions, with no cost implications, so that individual transmissions tend to be short and incomplete in character.

In the end, whatever the strengths and weaknesses of texting as a variety of language, it is in the classroom that matters need to be managed. If there are children who are unaware of the difference between texting and standard English, then it is up to teachers to make them aware. If there are children whose discourse skills are being hampered by texting, then it is up to teachers to show them how to improve. Some methods will work well and some will not. As the old song might have said, it's not what you teach but the way that you teach it. The point is made succinctly by Jill Attewell in a paper for *Literacy Today* in 2003:[16]

---

[15] Naomi Baron and Richard Ling, 'IM and SMS: a linguistic comparison', paper given at the International Conference of the Association of Internet Researchers, Toronto, October 2003.

[16] <http://www.literacytrust.org.uk/Pubs/attewell.html>

there are reports of examiners finding SMS abbreviations and slang in GCSE English papers. This is worrying, although enquiries should perhaps focus on how teachers have prepared their pupils for the examinations rather than on the students' use of mobile phones.

It would indeed be worrying if students entered an examination hall unaware of the difference between formal and informal English, or between standard and nonstandard English. Fortunately, all the evidence from examiners and others suggests that the vast majority of students are well aware of the difference, and do not use textisms in their writing.

The research findings are promising, but we do not yet know if the positive results will be replicated across all ability levels of children and all aspects of linguistic structure. And the emergence of these findings does not mean that we can be blasé about maintaining a balance between texting and other aspects of linguistic behaviour. For example, the use of the phone keypad, along with the ready availability of predictive texting, reinforces the point made in the 1990s that the internet is reducing the opportunities, and thus the ability, of children to use handwriting. Teaching – and examining – needs to take this into account. The need to maintain a clear and fluent handwriting style is of great importance – and not only to guard against the day when there is a power-cut.

Research reports also repeatedly draw attention to the reduced grammatical complexity of text messages – as indeed of some other kinds of electronic communication, such as chat and instant messaging. Text messages are quite short, compared with emails, blogging, and other kinds of forum activity, and certainly much shorter than most traditional forms of written expression, such as the letter, diary entry, or essay. The sentences are also shorter, making use of elliptical constructions in the manner of conversational speech (e.g. *Getting the 4 pm bus* rather than *I'm getting the 4 pm bus*). Grammatical words are often omitted, in the manner of a telegram (*bus arriving 7.10*). The danger here, it is suggested, is that the constraint to write in short sentences might make children think in correspondingly short bursts, so that they become less able to handle notions which require more complex elucidation. One of Veenal Raval's findings was that texters wrote less than non-texters when asked to describe a picture. If this turns out to be a genuine effect – that text messaging is fostering a reduction in discourse skills – then this is certainly something which needs to be compensated for in classroom activity. But findings are mixed. One research team found considerable collaborative discourse activity in using mobile phones, with young people often sitting together and exchanging text content in what they refer to as 'gift-giving rituals'.[17] And another study concluded that texting actually helps the development of communication skills such as the ability to summarize and express oneself concisely.[18] The same study also suggested that texting motivates people to sharpen their diplomatic skills, for, as with all written activity, it allows more time to formulate thoughts and express them carefully.

As with any new technology, people have to learn to manage it. There are undoubtedly problems in relation to the use of texting, but they seem to be social or physiological, not linguistic, in character. For example, one report, by Jan Van den Bulck from the Catholic University of Leuven in Belgium, found that text messages interrupted the sleep of most adolescents.[19] Among 13-year-olds, 13.4 per cent reported being woken up one to three times a month, 5.8 per cent were woken up once a week, 5.3 per cent were woken up several times a week, and 2.2 per cent were woken up every night. Among 16-year-olds, the interference was greater: 20.8 per cent were woken up between one and three times a month, 10.8 per cent were woken up at least

[17] A. S. Taylor and R. Harper, 'Age-old practices in the "new world": a study of gift giving between teenage mobile phone users', paper given at the Conference on Human Factors and Computing Systems, Minneapolis, April 2002.

[18] Kate Fox, 'Evolution, alienation and gossip: the role of mobile telecommunications in the 21st century', *Social Issues Research Centre, 2001.* <www.sirc.org/publik/gossip.shtml>

[19] Jan Van den Bulck, 'Text messaging as a cause of sleep interruption in adolescents, evidence from a cross-sectional study', *Journal of Sleep Research* 12 (2003), 263.

once a week, 8.9 per cent were woken up several times a week, and 2.9 per cent were woken up every night. This is an issue that goes well beyond the linguistic.

The issues raised by texting also go well beyond children in schools. Another report, by Glenn Wilson from the University of London, commissioned by technology firm Hewlett Packard, identified problems of reduced concentration, productivity, and even IQ among employees who spent too much time texting while at work.[20] The practice was evidently also causing some harm to personal relations: half the employees said they always responded immediately to a message – notwithstanding the fact that most people think it highly discourteous to read or answer a text message or email during a face-to-face meeting. The problems carried over into the outside world, with most employees reporting that they checked work-related text messages and emails even when at home or on holiday.

The press have made much use of the term 'addiction', when reporting such findings; and indeed, there have been reports of people booking themselves into clinics for help. In 2003 the Priory clinics were reporting a sharp rise in 'technology addiction', with some people evidently texting up to seven hours a day.[21] There have also been reports of undesirable physical effects. Physiotherapists have begun to notice cases of

---

[20] <http://www.timesonline.co.uk/tol/life_and_style/education/student/news/article 384086.ece>

[21] Report in <http://news.bbc.co.uk/1/hi/uk/3165546.stm>.

text message injury (TMI), a form of repetitive stress injury caused by excessive use of the thumb to type text messages.[22] There is also a risk of damage to the hand, wrist, and arm. They advise texters to use both hands when texting, to hold the phone higher up and as close to the body as possible to avoid neck and shoulder strain, to keep the phone as close to the body as possible to avoid extra strain on the arms, and to take regular breaks. Anything which reduces the number of keystrokes is seen as a good thing, such as predictive texting – or, of course, abbreviating.

At the same time, other reports are more positive. Texting has proved valuable in giving children a discreet way of reporting when they are being bullied.[23] Several teachers have stories of reserved, introverted, or nervous pupils who have had their expressive confidence boosted by their use of texting. The point has long been appreciated with reference to the use of the internet to provide chat forums in distance learning;[24] and it seems to be just as relevant here.

A national survey carried out by Kate Fox in 2001 for the Social Issues Research Centre in the UK drew attention to the important role played by texting as part

[22] <http://www.csp.org.uk/director/newsandevents/news.cfm?item_id=117F52FA BA0EFD81E11F1670148A480C>

[23] <http://www.bteducation.org/news/newsitem.ikml?id=376&PHPSESSID=13a35 84ee0>

[24] For example, by Boyd H. Davis and Jeutonne P. Brewer, *Electronic Discourse: Linguistic Individuals in Virtual Space* (Albany: State University of New York Press, 1997).

of the 'gossip' of a speech community.[25] Most of her focus-group participants saw texting as an important means of maintaining contact in a large social network:

> they found texting an ideal way to keep in touch with friends and family when they did not have the time, energy, inclination or budget for a 'proper' phone conversation or visit.

Her main conclusion in relation to the teenagers she interviewed supported the point made above:

> texting can help them to overcome their awkwardness and develop their social and communication skills: they communicate with more people, and communicate more frequently, than they did before having access to mobile texting.

Fox's conclusions about texting formed part of a larger study of the important role of gossip in maintaining social networks. Texting dialogue reminded her of village-green conversations where little content may be exchanged but personal connections are made. And the supporting technology for mobile phones has a similar social effect in other parts of the world. In Africa, for example, limited electricity supply has brought people together in an unexpected way:[26]

---

[25] See Fox (note 18).

[26] C. N. Adeya, 'Wireless technologies and development in Africa', in *Wireless Communication and Development: a Global Perspective*, 2005. <http://arnic.info/ workshop05.php>

In the town centre there is one phone shop that sells airtime and phones. This is where many people also charge their phones. Many have to wait for their phones because there have been incidents of phones disappearing, and there are no guarantees or insurances . . . It is common to find mostly professionals, like teachers, chatting near the shop as they wait because their schools do not have electricity; new social networks develop from this; discussions range from sharing expertise, development issues to politics . . .

[in another village] I have observed a few people who come specifically to charge their phones, mostly retirees who do not want to walk to the village shop, maybe to save their money and airtime. They are not charged for this but I have seen them discuss issues from their experience with those in the vicinity and others working in the compound like veterinarians and children. From a cultural aspect, it reminds me of how the old used to sit around the fire with the young and impart knowledge. This culture has gradually died in many communities but maybe this charging of mobile phones may partially replace it.

Texting is one of the most innovative linguistic phenomena of modern times, and perhaps that is why it has generated such strong emotions – 'a kind of laziness', 'an affectation', 'ridiculous'[27] – and why we

---

[27] <http://www.student.nada.kth.se/~u1slxvti/SPRAKT/sms.pdf>

have seen the 'moral panic' described in earlier chapters. Yet all the evidence suggests that belief in an impending linguistic disaster is a consequence of a mythology largely created by the media. Children's use of text abbreviations has been hugely exaggerated, and the mobile phone companies have played a part in this by emphasizing their 'cool' character, compiling dictionaries, and publishing usage guides – doubtless, thereby, motivating sales.

Texting has been blamed for all kinds of evils that it could not possibly have been responsible for. Virtually any piece of nonstandard English in schoolwork is now likely to be considered the result of texting, even if the evidence is incontrovertible that the nonstandardism has been around for generations. The other day I read about someone condemning *would of* (for *would have*) as a consequence of texting. That mis-spelling has been around for at least 200 years. You will find it in Keats. I have encountered similar misapprehensions in Japan, Finland, Sweden, and France, and it is probably present in every country where texting has become a feature of daily communication.

In a logical world, text messaging should not have survived. Imagine a pitch to a potential investor. 'I have this great idea. A new way of person-to-person communication, using your phone. The users won't have a familiar keyboard. Their fingers will have trouble finding the keys. They will be able to send messages, but with no more than 160 characters at a time. The writing on the screens will be very small and difficult to read, especially if you have a visual handicap. The messages will arrive at any time, interrupting your daily routine or your sleep. Oh, and every now and again you won't be able to send or receive anything because your battery will run out. Please invest in it.' What would you have done?

But, it was direct, avoiding the problem of tracking down someone over the phone. It was quick, avoiding the waiting time associated with letters and emails. It was focused, avoiding time-wasting small-talk. It was portable, allowing messages to be sent from virtually anywhere. It could even be done with one hand, making it usable while holding on to a roof-strap in a crowded bus. It was personal, allowing intimacy and secrecy, reminiscent of classroom notes under the desk. It was unnoticed in public settings, if the user turned off the ringtone. It allowed young people to overcome the spatial boundary of the home, allowing communication with the outside world without the knowledge of parents and siblings. It hugely empowered the deaf, the shared writing system reducing the gap between them and hearing people. And it was relatively cheap (though, given the quantity of messaging, some parents still had an unpleasant shock when their phone bill arrived). It wasn't surprising, therefore, that it soon became the preferred method of communication among teenagers. Youngsters valued its role both as a badge of identity, like accents and dialects, and as a ludic linguistic pastime. And in due course adults too came to value its discreetness and convenience. The interruption caused by the arrival of a text message is disregarded. To those who text, the beep heralding a new message invariably thrills, not pains.

How long will it last? It is always difficult to predict the future, when it comes to technology. Perhaps it will remain as part of an increasingly sophisticated battery of communicative methods, to be used as circumstances require. Or perhaps in a generation's time texting will seem as archaic a method of communication as the typewriter or the telegram does today, and new styles will have emerged to replace it. For the moment, texting seems here to stay, though its linguistic character will undoubtedly alter as its use spreads among the older population.

Some people dislike texting. Some are bemused by it. Some love it. I am fascinated by it, for it is the latest manifestation of the human ability to be linguistically creative and to adapt language to suit the demands of diverse settings. In texting we are seeing, in a small way, language in evolution.

Glossary

This glossary brings together the more specialized terms from mobile phone technology and from linguistics that I have used in this book, supplemented by a few other terms often encountered when investigating text messages.

abbreviation In texting, a reduced version of a word. The term **ellipsis** is used when sentences are shortened.

accommodation Adjustments which people make unconsciously to their speech or writing, influenced by the speech/writing of the person they are talking/writing to.

acronym A word made up out of the initial letters of other words. Some are pronounced letter-by-letter, such as *ftf* 'face to face'; these are also called **alphabetisms**. Some are pronounced as whole words, such as *lol* 'laughing out loud'.

bandwidth In acoustics, the interval between two given limits within which a range of frequencies falls. The notion defines the capacity of a channel to carry information without distortion.

bit An abbreviation of **Binary digIT**, a computational quantity with only two possible values in the binary number system, 0 or 1. All operations in digital computers and mobile phones take place by using a high or low voltage (an 'on' or 'off' state) to represent the binary digits.

blog An abbreviation for **Weblog** or **Web log**, an individual's frequently updated mixture of personal observation, commentary, and links posted as a Web page; the person who maintains such a log is a **blogger**, and the activity is known as **blogging**.

browser A type of computer program which uses the Internet to locate and transfer documents held on websites, and presents the documents to the user of the program in a way which makes them easy to read. Commonly used browsers are Internet Explorer, Mozilla Firefox, Safari, Opera, and Netscape.

byte A fixed number of bits (binary digits), usually defined as a set of 8 bits. An 8-bit byte can therefore take 256 different values corresponding to the binary numbers 00000000, 00000001, 00000010, through to 11111111.

cell In mobile communications, the geographical area where signals from a transmitter can be received. Mobile phone networks are typically made up of many cells each operating on a discrete frequency that will not interfere with those in use in adjacent cells. In a cellular network, a signal can be passed between cells, as a mobile phone conversation moves about; in a non-cellular network, phones are linked to a single (more powerful) transmitter.

cellphone, cell phone, cellular phone *see* **mobile phone**

character Any graphic unit in a writing system, such as a letter, punctuation mark, or special symbol (such as &). In a narrower sense, it refers to a graphic unit which represents a word or part of a word, such as the characters of Chinese or Japanese writing.

chat A mobile-phone messaging service offered by some service providers which enables users with suitably equipped phones to engage in point-to-point messaging between two users, or multi-point chat with several users simultaneously. It is also possible to access some Internet chat sites.

chatgroup, chat group A group of people who meet regularly at a particular Internet site (a **chatroom** or **chat room**) to discuss topics of common interest. Most chats take place in real time (they are *synchronous*), but it is possible to carry on a conversation in an *asynchronous* way, where the messages are stored for later scrutiny, as with bulletin boards and mailing lists.

clipping A word formed by leaving out the last letter or letters, such as *comin* for *coming*.

code-mixing In bilingual speech or writing, the transfer of linguistic elements (such as words or spellings) from one language into another, as when Italian *che* is written as *ke* (the *k* not being a letter of the Italian alphabet).

computer-mediated communication (CMC) The kind of language used when people talk to each other using electronic means.

content service In mobile communications, a paging service which goes beyond telephone-number alerts to include all kinds of information (**content**), such as news and sports headlines, personalized stock quotes, driving directions, and restaurant reviews.

contraction A word where letters have been omitted in the middle, such as *bt* for *but*. The term is also used for forms which are the result of two words coming together, as in *I'm* (= *I am*).

dlacritic A mark added to a written symbol, which alters the way it is pronounced in a language. Diacritics are usually omitted in texting.

dialect A variety of language in which the grammar and vocabulary identifies the regional, social, or occupational origins of the user.

download To transfer information from one kind of electronic storage to another, especially from a larger store to a smaller one, such as a file from a network onto a mobile phone; also, the information so transferred.

electronic discourse The kind of language used in computer-mediated communication, especially as found in dialogue situations such as email, chatgroups, or texting exchanges.

ellipsis A sentence where part of the structure has been omitted, such as *Going out tonight?* for *Are you going out tonight?* Many sentences in texting are **elliptical**.

email/e-mail or **electronic mail** The use of computer systems to transfer messages between individual users. Messages are usually stored centrally until accessed by the recipient.

emoticon or **smiley** A combination of keyboard characters designed to convey the emotion associated with a particular facial expression. They are typed as a string on a single line. The simplest forms represent basic attitudes: positive, in the case of :) and negative in the case of : (

geek Someone who is technically knowledgeable about computers and the Internet; also, anyone who spends a significant proportion of social (as opposed to professional) life online.

Global System for Mobile Communication (GSM) A standardization group set up in 1982 to define a common standard for mobile communications in Europe. The first commercial system began operating in 1991, and the standard has now become worldwide. GSM exists in three different versions: GSM 900 and GSM 1800 are used in Europe and Asia, and GSM 1900 is used in North America. Mobile-phone handsets are available which will work on all three bands (**tri-band** handsets).

grammar The study of the structure of sentences (**syntax**) and words (**morphology**).

grammatical words A word whose function is to express a grammatical relationship in a sentence, such as *the*, *it*, *of*, or *and*.

i-mode A wireless Internet service launched by the Japanese firm DoCoMo in 1999.

inflection A part of a word that signals a grammatical relationship, such as plural -*s* in English or past tense -*ed*.

initialism The reduction of a word to its initial letter, as in *v* for *very*.

instant message (IM) A type of email which informs the recipient the moment it arrives at a computer (instead of being left in an inbox to be discovered later), and thus permits rapid dialogue exchanges. The application which enables this to happen is an **instant messenger**.

Internet or Net (sometimes not capitalized) An association of computer networks with common standards which enable messages to be sent from any host on one network to any host on any other. It is now the world's largest computer network.

iPhone A mobile phone launched by Apple in the USA in 2007, which allows a wide range of multimedia and Internet functions as well as text messaging and visual voicemail.

keypad The set of alphanumeric push buttons on a mobile phone.

keypad lock A mobile-phone function which disables the push buttons on a handset, thus preventing calls being made accidentally.

keypad tones The sounds made when the push buttons on a mobile-phone handset are pressed.

lingua franca A language which is used to permit routine communication between groups of people who speak different languages. English is a global lingua franca and, as such, influences many texting practices.

linguistics The scientific study of language.

logogram A written symbol that represents a word or a meaningful part of a word (such as a prefix); also called a **logograph**, and (in certain languages, such as Chinese) a **character**.

ludic language Language whose primary function is to be playful.

macaronic Describing any piece of speech or writing which playfully mixes up two languages.

message alert tone The distinctive tone sounded by a mobile phone when a new text-message is received. On some phones, the tone can be personalized by the user.

messaging The transfer of a text message from a mobile handset or personal digital assistant to one or more persons via a mobile phone, pager, or other method.

mobile communications A system which provides a simple, convenient means of communication for people who wish to keep in touch when travelling. The first mobile communication system was ship-borne radio, and there have since been widespread developments in the field of military communications. In modern times the term also refers to personal communication systems such as CB radio, radio paging, and car and pocket phones which use cellular radio.

mobile phone or **mobile** (UK), **cellphone, cell phone** (US), also **cellular** A portable telephone handset, used with a cellular radio or other mobile communication system, small enough to fit into a pocket or bag. It enables users to make direct-dial telephone calls from any location within the service area of the network they have opted to use.

Multimedia Messaging Service (MMS) A technology which enables the delivery of voice, text, graphics, audio, and video to mobile phones.

orthography A standardized system for writing a language. It includes everything to do with spelling, capitalization, and punctuation.

pager Originally, a simple communications device that emitted a beep to alert the user to make contact with a caller, but later a device that could also receive and display short text messages. It is usually small enough to fit into a pocket.

pay as you go A payment scheme for mobile phones whereby the user purchases a certain amount of airtime in advance (prepaid) either by credit vouchers (available from many types of shops) or by credit/debit card payment online to the network operator.

pay monthly A payment scheme for mobile phones whereby a 12-month contract is agreed between the customer and a network operator, and payments (which include a fixed charge as well as call charges) are made monthly. The fixed charge normally includes some free airtime.

pay up front A payment scheme for mobile phones whereby a customer pays for 12 months' line rental in advance. The network in return offers a quantity of free airtime every month.

phatic communion The social function of language, used to show rapport between people or to establish a pleasant atmosphere. Many textisms involve a phatic function, such as *g* ('grin').

phonetic spelling A spelling system which represents speech sounds in a regular, one-to-one way. Many of the forms in texting are phonetic representations, such as *wot* for *what*.

pictogram A symbol used in picture-writing; also called a **pictograph**. Emoticons are a type of pictogram.

predictive texting or **T9** (from 'Text on 9 keys') A function which uses software and a database built into the mobile phone to predict the most likely word being entered as a user presses the keys. Only one key-press is required for each letter, and it is the sequence and combination of keys that determines the word displayed. If several words share a combination, the most frequently used word is displayed first and the user can either accept it or use a key to scroll through alternatives. Words can be added to the database.

profiles Functions which are used to personalize the features of a mobile handset. They include level of volume, type of ringtone, and message alert tone.

rebus Words and sentences made out of a combination of letters, pictures, or logograms, such as *c u l8r* 'see you later'.

reverse billing An emerging service offered by mobile-phone service providers whereby users can pay for products and services by adding the charge to their phone account or having the amount deducted from their prepaid credit. It is particularly aimed at a market sector where low-value or micro-payment transactions (pence or cents rather than pounds or dollars) are the norm.

ringtone The sound produced by a telephone when it receives an incoming call. A wide range of ringtones has evolved for mobile phones, to enable users to identify their own phone when it rings.

roaming The ability to operate a mobile phone on a different network from the one the user has subscribed to. If a mobile phone cannot connect to the network owned by the user's mobile service provider, it will attempt to connect to any other compatible network within range. The connection will only be accepted if the two networks have a **roaming agreement** and the user has made an appropriate arrangement. The phone companies will then exchange information about the usage, and the home operator will charge the user for the calls made and received on the other network. Roaming is more expensive than calls made through the home operator, and the user has to pay an extra charge for incoming calls.

scrolling The vertical displacement of information which occurs when reading a page that is larger than what can be seen on a single computer or mobile phone screen. New material appears at the bottom of the screen at the same rate as material at the top of the screen disappears.

Short Messaging Service (SMS) *see* **texting**

SIM card An abbreviation for **Subscriber Identity Module card**: a smart card that fits into a mobile phone and gives the user access to the mobile network. The SIM card contains a number of security functions, and it is possible to use it to save information such as names and telephone numbers.

SIM lock An abbreviation for **Subscriber Identity Module lock**: software that locks a phone to a specific SIM card and network. The phone will not work if a different SIM card is inserted.

smart messaging or **enhanced messaging service (EMS)** A mobile phone system which delivers text messages with a limited number of added features, such as business cards, or ringtone and profile downloads.

speed dialling or **one-touch dialling** A function available on many fixed and mobile-phone handsets that enables the user to store telephone numbers in numbered memory locations, then later to dial a selected telephone number using the much shorter location number.

standard language The variety of a language chosen by its speakers to act as an educated norm. It is chiefly identified in writing through the use of an agreed system of spelling, punctuation, and grammar. Departures from these norms are said to be **nonstandard** (some people use a more dismissive term, **substandard**). Textisms include some abbreviations that are also found in the standard language, such as *iou* or *asap*, but the vast majority are nonstandard.

stylistics The study of any situationally distinctive use of language, and of the choices made by individuals and social groups in their use of language. Also, the study of the way language is used for expressive or aesthetic effect.

texting or **text-messaging** A mobile phone service that enables a user to send short written messages to other mobile users. The service uses the control channels, which allows a message to arrive while a voice call is in progress, but limits the length of the message to a maximum of 160 characters.

textism An abbreviated word form that is distinctive in texting, such as *c* for *see*, *txt* for *text*, *jk* for *just kidding*, and *2day* for *today*. Some of these forms are used in other kinds of electronic communication.

textonyms The set of words which are generated by a single sequence of numerals keyed in to a mobile phone; also called **homonumeric words**. For example, *726* produces *pam*, *ram*, *sam*, and *ran*.

textspeak An informal name for the kind of abbreviated language used in text messaging, and sometimes for any kind of text messaging, whether abbreviated or not.

three-way calling, usually written **3-way calling** In mobile phone communications, a system that allows three parties to share a conversation.

vote exchanging A practice used in some website competitions which allows people to vote for the site you favour in exchange for you voting for theirs. The idea is similar to the 'pairing' system sometimes encountered in politics (e.g. 'I won't vote for X if you don't vote for Y'). Several competitions disallow it.

Web or **World Wide Web, WWW,** or **W3** An Internet facility designed for multimedia use, in which individuals or organizations make available 'pages' of information to other users. Technically, it is the full collection of all the computers linked to the Internet which hold documents that are mutually accessible through use of a standard protocol (the HyperText Transfer Protocol, or HTTP). The creator of the Web, British computer scientist Tim Berners-Lee, defined it as 'the universe of network-accessible information, an embodiment of human knowledge'. Anything that can exist as a computer file can be made available as a Web document – text, graphics, sound, video, etc. A further necessary element of the Web is the search engine, a means of locating documents by content rather than by location.

website A set of interconnected Web pages (documents transferable to and presented by browsers), usually located on a single computer server, and prepared and maintained as a collection of information by the site owner. Websites are identified by a unique address, or **URL** (**Uniform Resource Locator**).

English text abbreviations

This appendix contains a list of abbreviations which are said to be used in English text messages. See page 123ff. for a discussion.

Abbreviation	Meaning
@	at
1daful	wonderful
2	to, too, two
2b, 2B	to be
2d4, 2D4	to die for
2day, 2DAY	today
2moro	tomorrow
2nite	tonight
4	for, four
4e, 4ever	forever
8	ate (*or as part of word*)
a3	anytime, anywhere, anyplace
aam, aamof	as a matter of fact
ab	ah bless!
add	address

Abbreviation	Meaning
afaik	as far as I know
aisb	as I said before
aml	all my love
asl	age, sex, location
aslmh	age, sex, location, music, hobbies
atm	at the moment
atw	at the weekend
ax	across
b, B	be (*or as part of word*)
b4	before
b4n	bye for now
bbl	be back later
bbs	be back soon
bcnu	be seeing you
beg	big evil grin
bf	boyfriend
bg	big grin
bion	believe it or not
bn	been, being
brb	be right back
brt	be right there
btdt	been there, done that

English text abbreviations

Abbreviation	Meaning
btr	better
btw	by the way
c	see
c%d	could
c%l	cool
chln	chilling
cid	consider it done
cm	call me
cmb	call me back
cn	can
cu	see you
cupl	couple
cuz, cos	because
cya	see ya (= you)
d	the
d8	date
dinr	dinner
dk	don't know
doin	doing
dur	do you remember
ezi, ezy	easy

Abbreviation	Meaning
f	friend
f2t	free to talk
fc	fingers crossed
ff	friend(s) forever
fone	phone
ftbl	football
fwiw	for what it's worth
g	grin
g2g, gtg	got to go
g9	genius
gal	get a life
gbh	great big hug
gf	girlfriend
gl	good luck
gm	good move
gmab	give me a break
gr8	great
gt	good try
h2cus	hope to see you soon
h8	hate
hagn	have a good night

English text abbreviations

Abbreviation	Meaning
hak	hugs and kisses
hand	have a nice day
hbtu	happy birthday to you
hhoj	ha ha only joking
hig	how's it going
howru	how are you
hth	hope this helps
hv	have
iccl	I couldn't care less
icwum	I see what you mean
idk	I don't know
ilu, iluvu, ily, iluvy	I love you
imho	in my honest / humble opinion
imi	I mean it
imo	in my opinion
iooh	I'm outta here
irl	in real life
iuss, iyss	if you say so
j4f	just for fun
jam	just a minute
jk	just kidding

Abbreviation	Meaning
jtluk, jtlyk	just to let you know
kc	keep cool
khuf, khyf	know how you feel
kit	keep in touch
kwim	know what I mean
l8	late
l8r	later
lmao	laughing my ass off
lmk	let me know
lo	hello
lol	laughing out loud
luv	love
m8	mate
mbrsd	embarrassed
mob	mobile
msg	message
mtf	more to follow
n	and; no
n1	nice one
nagi	not a good idea
nc	no comment

Abbreviation	Meaning
ne	any
ne1	anyone
nethng	anything
no1	no one
np	no problem
nvm	never mind
o	or
omg	oh my God
ova	over
pcm	please call me
pita	pain in the ass
pls	please
ppl	people
prt	party
prw	parents are watching
ptmm	please tell me more
qix	quick
r	are
rgds	regards
rotfl	rolling on the floor laughing
sc	stay cool

Abbreviation	Meaning
sit	stay in touch
sme1	someone
sol	sooner or later
sot	short of time
spk	speak
sry	sorry
stats	your sex and age
sum1	someone
sup	what's up
swdyt	so what do you think
sys	see you soon
t+	think positive
t2go	time to go
ta4n, tafn	that's all for now
tcoy	take care of yourself
thn	then
thnq, thnx, thx, tx	thank you, thanks
tmb	text me back
tmi	too much information
toy	thinking of you
tttt, ttutt, ttytt	to tell (you) the truth

English text abbreviations

Abbreviation	Meaning
ttul, ttul8r, ttyl, ttyl8r	talk to you later
tuvm, tyvm	thank you very much
txt	text
u	you
u4c	yours for ever
uwot	you what
v	very
w	with
w8	wait
wadr	with all due respect
wan2	want to
wassup, wu, wuuu	what's up?
wayd	what are you doing
wbs	write back soon
wckd	wicked
wen, wn	when
wenja	when do you
werja	where do you
werru	where are you
werubn	where have you been
wk	week

Abbreviation	Meaning
wknd	weekend
wl	will
wot	what
wtf	what the fuck
wtm	what time?
wuwh, wywh	wish you were here
xlnt	excellent
y	why; yes
ya	you, your
ybs	you'll be sorry
yiu	yes I understand
yr, YR	your
yyssw	yeah, yeah, sure, sure – whatever
z	said

Text abbreviations in eleven languages

This appendix illustrates the way text abbreviations are used in eleven languages, and provides sources for a few more. English glosses are selective: they do not give all the meanings of a form in a language. See page 123 for the limitations of the material.

Chinese

Abbreviation	Full form (pinyin)	English gloss
+u	jia you	come on! (i.e. encourage)
555	wuwuwu	whimper
88	baibai	bye-bye
b4	bishi	despise [also 'before']
bb	baobei	darling, baby
bc	baichi	idiot
bs	bishi	despise
cm	choumei	show off
dd	didi	brother
ddd	dingdingding	agree
dx	daxia	expert
gg	gege	brother

Abbreviation	Full form (pinyin)	English gloss
jj	jiejie	sister
kl	konglong	dinosaur (ugly woman)
mm	meimei	sister
mpj	mapijing	flatterer
plmm	piaoliang meimei	pretty girl

Source: Liwei Jiao
Report of Ministry of Education and National Language Committee of China, 22 May 2006.

Czech

Abbreviation	Full form	English gloss
bo	nebot	because
cj	co je	what
csdd	co se dá dělat	well, it can't be helped
ctmb	co to má být	what's that supposed to mean
dh	drž hubu	shut up
dn	dobrou noc	good night
dyz	když	when, if
hh	ha ha	ha ha
hosipa	hovno si pamatuju	I can't remember anything
jj	jo jo	oh yes
jn	jo no	ok then
jsm	jak se máš	how are you
jszbz	já se z tebe zblázním	you're going to drive me mad
kkt	kokot	prick
kua	kurva	whore (*as swear word*)
mkc	musím končit, čau	have to go, bye
mmt, mmnt	moment	wait a moment
msf	měj se fajn	enjoy (*when saying goodbye*)
mt	miluji tě	I love you
mtm	moc tě miluju	I love you very much

Abbreviation	Full form	English gloss
mtr	mám tě rád	I love you (*less strong*)
nj	no jo	ok then
nn, ee	ne, ne	no, no
nvm	nevím	I do not know
nz	není zač	you're welcome (*after 'thank you'*)
o5	opět	again
o5z5	opět zpět	back again
omnm	odepiš mi na mobil	write me back on my mobile
phd	pohoda	everything ok
ptze, pze, ptz	protože	because
sem	jsem	I am
si	jsi	you are
srsm	sereš mě	you're a pain
szm	jsem zamilovaný	I'm in love
tj	to jo	that's right
tvl, twe	ty vole	mate, dude
vpho	v pohodě	that's ok
z5	zpět	back
zaves	žádný velký sraní	no big deal
zz	zatím zdar	bye for now

Source: Ivan Burda, Klara Strnadova

Dutch

Abbreviation	Full form	English gloss
&	en	and
2l8	te laat	late
b&	ben	am
blk	bleek	pale
d	de	the, that
dk	dat ik	that I
dt	dat	that
gl	geen	no
gep	geen enkel probleem	no problem
gkcht	gekocht	bought
gld	geld	money
hb	heb	have
ikvou	ik houd van je	I love you
ikwniet	ik weet niet	I don't know
j	je, jij, jou	you
k	ik	I
khb	ik heb	I have
kmn	komen	come
kmt	komt	comes
kn	kan	can

Abbreviation	Full form	English gloss
krgt	krijgt	gets
lf	lief	dear
m, mn	mijn	my
mgge	morgen	morning
mkn	maken	make
mr, ma	maar	but
n, 1	een	one
ngd8	nagedacht	thought
nr	naar	to, at
nt	niet	not
nwe	nieuwe	new
ok	ook	too
oppt	oppie toppie	just perfect
ovr	over	about, over
r	er	there
s	is	is
tis	het is	it is
v, vn	van	of, from
vl	veel	much
vm	van mij	from me
vor, vr	voor	before, for

Text abbreviations in eleven languages

Abbreviation	Full form	English gloss
vrdr	verder	further
vrlfd	verliefd	in love
wrm	warm	warm
zvl	zoveel	so much

Source: Lucy Crystal, Leander Huizinga, Jon Matthews <http://www.onzetaal.nu/finalisten.php>
E. A. Mante and D. Piris, 'El uso de la mensajeria movil por los jovenes en holanda', *Revista de Estudios de Juventud* 57 (2002), 47–58. <http://www.injuve.mtas.es/injuve/contenidos.item.action?id=149095362&menuId=1969776808>

Finnish

Abbreviation	Full form	English gloss
al	akku loppuu	the battery is running out
aun	älä unta nää	dream on
eos	en osaasanoa	can't tell you
et	ei todellakaan	impossible
evvk	ei vois vähempää kiinnostaa	don't give a damn
evy	en voi ymmärtää	don't understand
hih	hihitän itseni hengliltä	laughing to hell
hk	henkilökohtainen	personal
hy	hyvää yötä	good night
jks	järjen käyttö sallittua	common sense permitted
miso	missä olet?	where are you
misume	miten sulla menee	how are you
mrs	minä rakastan sinua	I love you
tmy	tule meille yöksi	will you come back for the night
tt	terkkua tutuille	greetings to all

Source: V. Oksman and P. Rautiainen, 'Toda mi vida en la palma de mi mano: la communicacion movil en la vida diaria de niños y adolescentes de Finlandia', *Revista de Estudios de Juventud* 57 (2002), 25–32. <http://www.injuve.mtas.es/injuve/contenidos.item.action?id=149095362&menu Id=1969776808>

French

Abbreviation	Full form	English gloss
@2m1, a2m1	à demain	till tomorrow
1	un	one
6né	ciné	cinema
a12C4	à un de ces quatres	see you one of these days
alp	à la prochaine	bye-bye for now
amha	à mon humble avis	in my humble opinion
apls, @+	à plus	see you later
asv	âge, sexe, ville	age, sex, location
auj	aujourd'hui	today
b1sur	bien sûr	of course
bcp	beaucoup	very much
bi1to	bientôt	soon
bjr	bonjour	good day
bsr	bonsoir	good evening
c, cé	c'est	it is
cad	c'est-à-dire	that is
cb1	c'est bien	that's good
c cho	c'est chaud	it's hot
ché	chez	at the home of

Abbreviation	Full form	English gloss
chu, chui, chuis	je suis	I am
c mal1	c'est malin	that's sneaky
c pa 5pa	c'est pas sympa	that's not nice
cpg	c'est pas grave	it's not bad
ct	c'était	it was
d	de	of
d100	descend	get down
dak, d'ac	d'accord	ok
dqp	dès que possible	as soon as possible
dsl	désolé	sad
edr	écroulé de rire	laughing out loud
entk, entouk	en tout cas	in any case
fds	fin de semaine	weekend
ght2v1	j'ai acheté du vin	I bought some wine
gr	gros	large
GspR b1	j'espère bien	I hope so
gt	j'étais	I was
jé, g	j'ai	I have
je c	je sais	I know
je le saV	je le savais	I knew it
jenémar	j'en ai marre	I'm sick of it
je t'm	je t'aime	I love you

Text abbreviations in eleven languages

Abbreviation	Full form	English gloss
je vé, j'vé	je vais	I'm going
jms	jamais	never
kand, kan	quand	when
kdo	cadeau	gift
ke	que	that, what
kel	quel, quelle	which
keske	qu'est-ce que	what
ki	qui	who
koi	quoi	what
lckc	elle s'est cassée	she left
lut, slt	salut	hi
mdr	mort de rire	rolling on the floor laughing
mr6	merci	thanks
msg	message	message
nsp	ne sais pas	dunno
o	au	in the, at the
ok1	aucun	none
oqp	occupé	busy
oué	ouais	yeah
parske	parce que	because
p-ê, pitit	peut-être	maybe

Abbreviation	Full form	English gloss
pkoi	pourquoi	why
po, pa	pas	not
qq	quelques	some
qqn	quelqu'un	someone
queske, q-c q	qu'est-ce que	what
koi29	quoi de neuf	what's new
raf	rien à faire	nothing to do
ras	rien à signaler	nothing to report
rdv	rendez-vous	date
re	retour, rebonjour	I'm back
ri1	rien	nothing
savapa	ça va pas	is something wrong
stp	s'il te plaît	please
svp	s'il vous plaît	please
t	t'es	you are
tabitou	t'habites où	where do you live
tt	t'étais	you were
ti	petit	little
tjs	toujours	always
tkc	t'es cassé	you're tired
tlm	tout le monde	everyone
t nrv	t'es énervé	are you irritated

Text abbreviations in eleven languages

Abbreviation	Full form	English gloss
tok	t'es ok	are you ok
toqp	t'es occupé	are you busy
vl	viens	come
vas-y	vazi	go
vrman	vraiment	really
vx	veux	want
x	crois, croit	believe
ya	il y a	there is/are

Source: <http://french.about.com/library/writing/bl-texting.htm>
See also: Cédrick Fairon, Jean René Klein, and Sébastien Paumier, *Le langage sms* (Louvain-la-Neuve: Presses universitaires de Louvain, 2007).

German

Dich ('you') and initial letters of nouns are often capitalized, and invariably so in standard German; only lower-case variants are shown here.

Abbreviation	Full form	English gloss
3n	nie, niemals, nirgendwo	no way, no how
3st	das war dreist	that was cheeky
8ung	achtung	attention
anws	auf nimmerwiedersehn	for good and all
baba	bye-bye	bye-bye
bbb	bis bald, baby	see you soon, baby
bihoba	bis hoffentlich bald	hope to see you soon
bild	bärchen, ich liebe dich	baby, I love you
bs	bis später	see you later
dad	denk an dich	thinking of you
dbee	du bist ein engel	you're an angel
dbmtm	du bist mein traummann	you're my dream man
dg	dumm gelaufen	shit happens
div	danke im voraus	thanks in advance
ff	fortsetzung folgt	to be continued
fg	fett grins	big grins
g	grinsen	grin
gn8	gute nacht	good night
guk	gruß und kuß	love and kisses

Text abbreviations in eleven languages

Abbreviation	Full form	English gloss
hdal	habe dich auch lieb	love you too
hdl	habe dich lieb	love you
hdlas	hast du lust auf sex	fancy some sex
hdlfiue	habe dich lieb für immer und ewig	love you now and forever
hdml	habe dich mega lieb	love you lots
hdos	halt die ohren steif	keep a stiff upper lip
idad	ich denk an dich	I'm thinking of you
ild, ily	ich liebe dich	I love you
itvd	ich träum von dir	I'm dreaming of you
ka	keine ahnung	no idea
kb	korrespondenz beendet	message ends
kd	knuddel dich	cuddling you
khzm	kommste heut zu mir	come out with me today
kk	kein kommentar	no comment
lamito	lache mich tot	laughing myself to death
ldnu	lass dich nicht unterkriegen	stand your ground
lg	liebe grüße	kind regards
lidumi?	liebst du mich?	do you love me
mad	mag dich	love you
mdt	mag dich trotzdem	still love you

Abbreviation	Full form	English gloss
mfg	mit freundlichen grüßen	with best wishes
mwn	meines wissens nicht	not to my knowledge
nok	nicht ohne kondom	not without condom
pg	pech gehabt	bad luck
sofa	sonntagsfahrer	Sunday driver
ß	schreib zurück	write soon
ssz	schreib schnell zurück	write back soon
stn	schönen tag noch	have a good one
tabu	tausend bussis	thousand kisses
tml	tut mir leid!	sorry
ts	träume süss	sweet dreams
uawg	um antwort wird gebeten	RSVP
wdmmg	willst du mit mir gehen	will you come out with me
we	wochenende	weekend
widmihei	willst du mich heiraten	will you marry me
www	wir werden warten	we'll wait

Source: <http://www.absmsen.de/index.html> (the section headed SMS-Abkürzungen)

Italian

Abbreviation	Full form	English gloss
+ −	più o meno	more or less
anke	anche	also
c sent	ci sentiamo	see you later
cmq	comunque	anyhow
dm	domani	tomorrow
dp	dopo	after
dr	dire	say
dv 6	dove sei	where are you
dx	destra	right
frs	forse	perhaps
ke	che	what, that
ki	chi	who
km	come	how
kn	con	with
ks	cosa	thing
−male	meno male	luckily
mmt+	mi manchi tantissimo	I miss you very much
nm	numero	number
nn	non	not
prox	prossimo	next

Abbreviation	Full form	English gloss
qlk	qualche	some
qlk1	qualcuno	someone
qlks	qualcosa	something
qnd	quando	when
qndi	quindi	therefore
qnt	quanto	how much
qst	questo	this one
rsp	rispondi	reply
scs	scusa	excuse
sl	solo	only
smpr	sempre	always
sms	messaggio	message
sn	sono	are
spr	sapere	know
sx	sinistra	left
sxo	spero	I hope
t tel + trd	ti telefono più tardi	I'll phone you later
trnqui	tranquillo	calm
trp	troppo	too much
tvtb	ti voglio tanto bene	I like you very much
xché, xké, xk	perché	why, because
xciò	perciò	therefore

Text abbreviations in eleven languages

Abbreviation	Full form	English gloss
xò	però	but
xsona	persona	person
xxx	tanti baci	lots of kisses

Source: <http://italian.about.com/od/vocabulary/a/aa053106a.htm>

Portuguese

Abbreviation	Full form	English gloss
−	menos	less
+	mais	more
+−	mais ou menos	more or less
=	igual	same
aki	aqui	here
al	almoço	lunch
bjs	beijos	kisses
c, c/	com	with
c/o	como	how
cel	celular	cellphone
d	de	of
d+	demais	besides
dn, dnd	de nada	don't mention it
dzr	dizer	say
eleg	elegante	smart
esp	especial	special
fig	figura	figure
gd	grande	big
hj	hoje	today
jt	jantar	dinner

Text abbreviations in eleven languages

Abbreviation	Full form	English gloss
kf	café	coffee
ksa	casa	house
mas	massa	money
msg	mensagem	message
msm	mesmo	same
mt, mto	muito	very
ñ, n, na	não	no, not
obg, tks, thx	obrigado	thanks
p	por	by, for
p/	para	for, through
pc	pouco	little
plz, pls	por favor	please
pq	porque	because
q, k	que	that, which
qdo	quando	when
qq	qualquer	any
saud	saudade	longing
sg	significa	means
sup	surpresa	surprise
tb	também	also
tc	teclar	key in
tdb	tudo de bom	all's well

Appendix B

Abbreviation	Full form	English gloss
tiamu, ily, ilu	te amo	I love you
to	estou	are
vamu	vamos	let's go
vc	você	you
x	vez	time

Source: Francisco Gomes de Matos, Madson Diniz, Andre Padilha, Tony Berber Sardinha
<http://ajuda.sapo.pt/comunicacao/sms/utilizacao_do_servico/Dicion_rio_de_abreviaturas_SMS.
html>
<http://veja.abril.com.br/idade/exclusivo/jovens_2003/sms.html>
See also: Joviana Benedito, *Dicionário para Chat, SMS e E-mail* (Lisbon: Edições Centro Atlântico,
2003).

Spanish

Abbreviation	Full form	English gloss
−	no	no, not
+	más	more
+tikr	masticar	chew
0/ning	ninguno	no-one
a2	adiós	goodbye
aa	años	years
b	beso	kiss
bstnt	bastante	enough
cia	compañía	company
comnikr	comunicar	report
complikdo	complicado	complicated
d	de	of
dcir	decir	say
dd	días	days
dir	dirección	direction
do	domingo	Sunday
exclnt	excelente	excellent
fsta	fiesta	festival
fvor	favor	please
garntzr	garantizar	guarantee

Abbreviation	Full form	English gloss
gf, jf	jefe	chief
gnt	gente	people
gr, thx	gracias	thanks
gral	general	general
gralmnt	generalmente	generally
hab	habitación	room
hcer	hacer	make
hl	hola	hello
hno	hermano	brother
hr	hora	time
kpaz	capaz	able
kro	caro	dear
lgr	lugar	place
mjr	mejor	better
mm	meses	months
mñna, mñn, mnna, mnn	mañana	tomorrow
msj, sms	mensaje	message
msjr	mensajero	messenger
nd	nada	nothing
nka	nunca	never
pers	personas	persons
prblm	problema	problem

Text abbreviations in eleven languages

Abbreviation	Full form	English gloss
prpar2	preparados	ready
q	que	what
qn	quien	who
qndo	cuando	when
s	ese	that
s3	estrés	stress
salu2	saludos	greetings
st	este	this
t2	todos	all
tb	también	also
tq	te quiero	I love you
tx	taxi	taxi
txt	texto	text
x	por	for
xa	para	for, to
xfa	por favor	please
xq	porque	because
xtrangro	extranjero	foreign

Source: <http://www.oup.com/uk/booksites/content/0198604750/resources/spanish_sms>

Swedish

Abbreviation	Full form	English gloss
3vlig	trevlig	nice
7k	sjuk	sick
asg	asgarv	big laugh
bsdv	bara så du vet	just so you know
cs	ses	see you
d	du/dig/din/det	you, it
d1a	detta	this
dt	det	it
e, r	är	is
eg	egentligen	really
f1	fett	cool
fr	från	from
hare	ha det bra	take care
iaf	i alla fall	in any case
iofs	i och för sig	actually
ivf	i varje fall	anyhow
lixom	liksom	like
lr, elle	eller	or
mkt	mycket	much
ngn, nön	någon	someone

Text abbreviations in eleven languages

Abbreviation	Full form	English gloss
ngt	någonting	something
o, oxå, åxå	också	also
pok, p&k	puss och kram	kiss and hug
ql	kul	fun
r	är	are
t	tid	time
tfn	telefon	phone
tkr	tycker	think
x	puss	kiss

Source: Suzanne Hugoson

Welsh

Abbreviation	Full form	English gloss
?wt	ble wyt ti	where are you
@b	ateb	answer
@ch	atoch	to you
@f	ataf	to me
@t	atat	to you
0	dim	not
01ia2	dymuniadau	wishes
01ia2 A1	dymuniadau gorau	best wishes
0N10	dim yn deg	not fair
1ig	unig	only
1ryw1	unrhyw un	anyone
8nosa	wythnosau	weeks
9	nain	gran
9r	nawr	now
bath	rhywbeth	something
bo	bod	be
bxo	becsio	worry
cal	cael	have
cdb	cau dy ben	shut up
cmru m bth	Cymru am Byth	Wales for ever

Text abbreviations in eleven languages

Abbreviation	Full form	English gloss
d	wedi	after
d1	wedyn	afterwards
fo	hefo	with
g3	gartre	home
gneud, gnd	gwneud	do
gt, oo	gweld ti	see you
gtd1, gtw	gweld ti wedyn	see you later
gwbo	gwybod	know
hlo	helo	hello
iwn	iawn	well
lla	efallai	perhaps
m	am	for
m8a	mwytha	cuddles
m8o	mwytho	cuddle
ma	mae	is
mav, MaV	dyma fi	here I am
mel	meddwl	think
mnd	mynd	go
mn nw	maen nhw	they are
n	yn	in
N2 (3,4,5, etc)	ein dau	one, two, etc.
n2 (3,4,5, etc)	ni'n dau	us two, etc

Abbreviation	Full form	English gloss
nw	enw	name
odd	oedd	was
pa	paid a	don't
pbl	pobol	people
pll	pell	far
Q	cyw	chick
r	ar	on
rbennig	arbennig	special
ryw1	rhywun	someone
sio	eisiau	want
smai, sumai	sut mae?	how are you
st, su	sut	how
su	sydd	is
sxi	secsi	sexy
t	ti	you
tav, TaV	ti a fi	you and me
tcso	tecstio	text
tiv, TiV	ti i fi	you to me
v	fi	me
w	wyt	you are
xxx	swsus	kisses

Source: <http://www.bbc.co.uk/cymru/radiocymru/c2/gwybodaeth/tecstio.shtml>

Other languages

<http://community.livejournal.com/linguaphiles/
3361181.html>
<http://www.telefonguru.hu/sms/sms_roviditesek.asp>

Index

Portland Community College